VIOLET AREVALO

THE MOST PRACTICAL
IMMIGRATINGAND**JOB HUNTING**
SURVIVAL GUIDE

proven simple steps to success

without the fears and doubts

THE MOST PRACTICAL
IMMIGRATING AND JOB HUNTING
SURVIVAL GUIDE
proven simple steps to success
without the fears and doubts

Bolet Arevalo

Cover Design by Patrick Lorenzo Arevalo

ISBN 10: 1-933817-69-0
ISBN 13: 978-1-933817-69-9

Published by Profits Publishing
http://profitspublishing.com/

US Address
1300 Boblett Street,
Unit A- 218
Blaine WA, 98230

Canadian Address
1265 Charter Hill Drive
Coquitlam, BC, V3E 1P1

Phone: 866-492-6623
Fax: 250-493-6603

Phone: 604-941-3041
Fax: 604-944-7993

Dedication

Immigrating and job hunting abroad are not exactly the first topics I wanted to write about. But after what I went through in the two years after I landed as an immigrant, I felt it was my moral duty to share my thoughts and the best lessons of carving a life in a strange country that many also dream to have. I do not consider myself at any high point of success as of yet but having hurdled the first two most challenging years, I believe the road ahead will be less difficult.

I am inspired by the tenacity of my own people who continue to dream and work out a better life abroad. This book is my tribute to them.

My family watches quietly on the side but they never fail to admire my constancy and same tenacity. I want this book to forever remind them that I persevere because I love them.

All my friends, social networkers or non-networkers alike, who send a word or two of encouragement all the time. I hope they find the real me in this book and continue to love me for who I am.

My friends in my new country, whose stories of struggle and triumph made me believe that there is always light at the end of the tunnel. Many of them never knew me from Adam, yet they embraced me and opened their hearts. With this book, I want to continue to discover with them the happiness of gathering little victories one day at a time.

Many times we wonder how much better life could be for people who move abroad. The one thing I know is—how much larger faith can grow with each day spent praying and praising God for His guidance and steadfast love. I offer this work to my Lord Jesus Christ and my fellow believers—that more than any riches in this world, the leaps and bounds that our faith grows in any journey is all that matters.

bolet

Special Thanks To My Vancouver Community

Tatay Tom, his MultiCultural Helping House Society and its staff, and the South Vancouver Neighborhood House for unreservedly welcoming St. Patrick's Parish and St. Patrick's Elementary School for accepting

BC MLA Mable Elmore for trusting

UBC Prof. Nora Angeles for believing

Tito Demi and Ate Rose for praying

Kuya Art and Ate Lilian for embracing

Linda and Lin for caring and encouraging

Kwangyoung and Donna for persisting

Classmates Amy and Nini for pushing

Dwayne and Lani for opening the door

Alex and Rowena for sharing their home

Al and Luna for kindly understanding

Jean and Ryan for willingly supporting

Bel and Lasalle for constantly listening

Norma and Caty for everything.

Introduction

I have intended this book to be as down-to-earth as possible while still remaining a feel-good piece of literature. The objective is not lofty. I just want it to enlighten, guide, comfort, reassure, stir hope and strengthen faith on a decision already made or about to be made.

I do not write in pretence of an authoritative or scholarly knowledge of the legalities, technicalities or even the proper psychology of living a dream away from one's home country. But it is my wish that every person who reads, browses or even just scans the pages of this book will encounter a personal message, a message that will leave a powerful impression in his heart—that if he is in the place of his true destiny, he can believe even that which he has not seen.

Destiny is where you are. What you will be is the result of what you do where you are.

That is how simple I have looked at this journey. Yet living these words meant learning to put behind every trace of where I had been and who I used to be. And that to me was painful, really painful.

When the provisions I had brought with me wore away every day, I found myself grappling for courage, for strength, for hope to continue moving forward. I felt that at that point, I had been broken. But I was not to be destroyed. I was shattered, but I have not fallen apart. I was crushed, but I can never be ruined.

Finding my writing has been my healing.

Writing has always been my first love. Yet, because I knew it would always be there, I was not able to give it time. Unfortunately, sometimes the same is true for family. Because we know they will always be there, we tend to trust that they always understand why they cannot see us 99 percent of the time.

If there is anything at all, my migration has changed that. Having led a pretty successful and gorgeous life back home, I must admit that it had been hard to even imagine having so much time on my hands and not knowing what to do. But my good friends knew that not doing anything was too unlike me. True enough, pretty soon, I realized that there was so much to do and to discover. And I had decided that before everything got out of hand again, I had to devote time to some serious writing.

It took me 15 weeks to finish my manuscript, actually 2 weeks behind my own target schedule. Still, I would like to think this was not bad for someone who had not done any serious writing in years. There were so many topics that I wanted to write about, but I thought that my migration to Canada must be of great consequence. I believe it is my present destiny.

I would not allow my first two years as an immigrant slip by me without documenting what had happened—not for my own sake, but for the sake of those who had just come over or for those who are coming after me.

Initially, I thought it was for the sake of others that I was writing about this topic. But as I was writing and going through the same problems, I was sometimes driven to tears at seeing how God could be so good that my writing helped to soothe every pain and frustration I felt deep within me. Writing this book has been therapeutic.

Finding yourself alone in a strange country can be so humbling that were it not for your Dream and Faith, you would never make it. They say the first two years are the most challenging. You need to be able to survive those two years, or you may find yourself trapped in unhappiness or wanting to just go back to your country of origin.

My book deals with these two challenging years, my first two years and how I survived.

I have organized this book into twenty chapters. The first ten chapters talk about the act of migrating and the next ten chapters tackle the crucial process of finding employment in a strange country. While time and again, I make reference to my experiences in my host country, I have endeavoured to speak from a point of view of somebody who can be anywhere in the world and needing guidance so that they, too, can survive their most challenging years.

There are two bonus write-ups that I am sharing in this book. The first one talks about what I believe are the ten reasons why an immigrant finds it difficult to get a job. I intend to use this article to set the tone and context of Chapters 11-20, which tackle the job search process.

The other write-up was a surprise even to myself because I did not know how my own job hunting would turn out and, therefore, how my book will conclude. I had not found a job even as I was writing my book, but nevertheless faithfully applied the lessons that I was sharing. I simply believed in my heart that my book will have a happy conclusion.

Towards the last 3 chapters, I got a job. And as I was concluding the last chapter, I was employed in the industry where I had been trained and spent the most productive years of my working life back in my home country. The best part was getting a chance to join a company consistently awarded as one of Canada's Top 50 Employers.

Believing that which you have not seen is the basis of my Christian faith. And that is how I was able to happily conclude my book.

Happy reading!

TABLE OF CONTENTS

CHAPTER 1   LEAVE EVERYTHING BEHIND

1.1   So, You're Leaving, Why?

> WHATEVER YOUR REASON FOR LEAVING, IT MUST MATTER MUCH TO YOU PERSONALLY AND THAT MUST BE CLEAR.

Your journey to finding a job in a new country begins with your decision to migrate, and so I am starting with this thought.

Sometimes, some good things in your life are not necessarily part of your dreams. They just happen. Migrating was not a dream for me.

I remember having told a friend shortly before I left that, as a child, I do not remember dreaming for myself. I came to where I am and became what I am simply by sheer design of an Unseen Hand. That was probably how my life had been laid out for me from the time I was born into this world.

All I know is that I kept on studying, studying till I excelled. I did not have the slightest idea of where I wanted to end up or what I would become. But even in the absence of a plan or an ambition, good education will most likely get you to something good. Things should work out well, so sometimes you just need to go with the flow.

But motherhood, or parenthood, has a way of changing that passive belief. As soon as you have children, things are different. Children send their own messages, just as children bring their own provisions. When I was getting really worried that I was having lots of children, a friend told me, "Every child brings his own bread." I always try to remember that.

Single people also have their own reasons to leave. In some cultures, the single ones are burdened even more greatly because they have to think about the future of their parents, their brothers and sisters, their nephews and nieces, and finally themselves. You leave to have a better life, whether you are a parent, unattached with a dependant, or simply single wanting to see more doors of opportunities open up.

There are real, good reasons why people go. The "better life" script may sound academic, but think about being given the chance to start a new life, to see another part of the world, know and understand other cultures, to encounter other possibilities in life, to rediscover yourself, to go back to school, to learn a new trade, or to meet your dream girl or guy.

Whatever the reason could be, the most important thing is, that reason should be CLEAR to you.

Packing your bags, resigning from a good job you love, leaving good friends and family behind, not being able to eat or see what you have always enjoyed. Whether or not you had a good job, leaving simply means turning your back on a lot of things and people.

Thus, your reason for leaving must be COMPELLING.

When I decided to leave, notwithstanding the seemingly heroic reason for doing so, I had to enumerate my own reasons for leaving, the possibilities I could look forward to for my own self. Surprisingly, I found more than one such reasons or possibilities.

My reason for thinking about those possibilities was simple: I was not about to sulk when I got to my new country or blame my own children or other people for getting depressed or losing in the next chapter of my life, both personally and professionally.

1. *People leave for a reason or reasons.*
2. *The reason or reasons must be clear to you.*
3. *There must be a reason that is personal to you, no matter how compelling the other reasons can be.*

1.2　　　Do You Know What to Bring And What Not to Bring?

ONLY WHEN YOU DECIDE TO LEAVE EVERYTHING BEHIND, AND KNOW THERE IS NO PLACE TO MOVE BUT FORWARD, THAT YOU CAN HOPE TO FIND THAT JOB OR THAT NEW LIFE AND NOT FOR A MOMENT THINK OF QUITTING.

With the recession, oil crisis and all, it is literally getting more and more difficult to be packing a lot when you go. You can only be allowed two 23-kilo pieces of luggage on the plane and one 13-kilo carry-on.

That's the case unless you have the money. You can actually ship out all your valuable possessions from your country when you leave or even at an indefinite later date as long as you inform the border authorities upon landing. At least that is true in Canada.

But how do you really decide what to bring and what not to bring? I once asked a friend if he were banished on an island, what was the one thing among his valuables that he would want to bring. He got mad at my question and bargained for at least five.

When you migrate, you certainly need to bring important documents. These I will not discuss because you are supposed to know that or will learn that somewhere else.

Secondly, you need to bring basic provisions, and enough not to need to buy them at dollar cost, when the money you are bringing in that you earned in your local currency has probably shrunk after being converted to the almighty dollar. Basic provisions are like the right clothes to bundle up, comfortable shoes, blankets to warm the nights, over-the counter first aid medicines, personal hygiene stuffs and the like.

Leaving as a family is more complicated and actually more stressful—physically, emotionally, provisionally and all. The mother or the father, or whoever has volunteered or naturally come out as virtual decision-maker on the packing job has got a really tough job ahead. I should know, I was that person. Packing took a year or so. As soon as we were certain of the approval to go, the process started and did not end until on the night before we left.

As I said, if there are enough funds to spend, then you can just decide to bring everything, call an international shipper and presto, your job is done. Of course, that is not usually the case. Even if you have the money, you might want to scrimp so that you have cash to dip into while you look for a job.

The other complication is that not all you have back home can be packed into a box or luggage, bundled up or shipped out. Some things are probably not practical to bring with you. There's the house, the car, the large appliances, the beautiful garden, your pets. What do you do with them?

Back home, I remember having an impromptu conversation with an older lady while waiting in line for a bank transaction. She said she was a retired government employee and that all her children live abroad. Quickly, there was something to talk about and I casually mentioned to her that my family was also migrating. Hearing that, she gave me an unsolicited advice, "When you leave, leave everything behind."

"Do you know why people do not succeed abroad, and therefore, are not happy?" she asked.
It is because they leave with this thought at the back of their minds, "If I do not make it here, I still have a house to go back to, my boss told me I can come back to my job anytime, etc." Any little frustration that comes their way emboldens them to quit because they have this house, this promise from the boss to pick up again, etc."

1. *You may choose to bring all your possessions if you can afford it.*

2. *Those that are physically impossible to bundle up prove to be the hardest to leave behind. But leave them anyway.*
3. *When finding the job you want is difficult, it is easier to not quit if you have decided to leave everything in your home country behind.*

1.3   **Are You Bringing What is Most Important?**

> ALTHOUGH YOU CANNOT PACK OR BUNDLE IT UP, YOU CAN AND YOU SHOULD BRING THE DREAM THAT MADE YOU DECIDE TO LEAVE. THAT DREAM SHOULD BE STRONG ENOUGH TO HELP YOU GET BY EVERY DAY AS YOU STRUGGLE TO FIND A JOB.

You can literally leave everything behind, but we all know that you can never, never leave whatever is ingrained in your mind or etched in your heart.

Be that as it may, make sure there will be no reason for you to want to quit and go back home in the face of even the slightest failure or frustration in your search for a job or a new life somewhere else.

It is not easy to start anew, but it is easy to quit. What makes quitting easier is the fact that you have options to go back to, and quite conveniently at that. You may not agree, but I think if you have these options even at the back of your mind, it is an indication that you are not that determined or serious in your decision to migrate.

When you travel even as tourist, the more organized and systematic among us usually come up with a checklist. This checklist includes things to bring, to buy, to settle, to pay, places to visit and people to call. The list is as huge as you yourself, with the certain age range you belong in, your civil status, the size of your family, and your clan or professional circle. The Canadian immigration procedure, for example, extends this list to asking you to determine what to bring now and what to bring later or to follow among what you possess now.

When you do the checklist, you will realize how cumbersome it can be. Or perhaps, how mushy. It is as if your whole life flashes back before you. As you sort your valuables, may be you will find your son's first teddy bear or the first Barbie doll your Dad gave you. And the temptation is to bring all these "firsts." The opposite is also true. Anything that reminds you of pain or anger is the first to travel to the trash can, never to be seen again.

There are more than a dozen things you can't even pack in that suitcase or box. The calls to make, the debts to settle, the people to see, the places to revisit. These things you cannot pack or bring with you are the intangibles. But don't forget to bring the only intangible that will make you persevere to search for a job, start a new life—your dream, your dream for yourself, for your children, for your parents, for your brothers and sisters, for your loved ones, including friends and partners.

As the song goes, that is your quest, to follow that star, no matter how hopeless, no matter how far…that dream can carry you.

1. *A checklist will help you manage your packing task.*
2. *Your checklist should include the intangibles, best of all that Dream.*
3. *Your Dream will certainly see you through that quest for that elusive job.*

1.4   Will You Burn Bridges?

WITH TECHNOLOGY AND ALL, IT IS SO EASY TO BE CONNECTED, SO DO NOT BURN YOUR BRIDGES. IT SURE FEELS BETTER TO WALK ON KNOWING THERE IS A BRIDGE THAT YOU CAN GO BACK AND FORTH OVER.

Leave everything behind, but do not burn bridges.

Do not burn the bridges that can warm your heart, inspire you, help you, support you or simply make you smile. The older you get to this stage of having to migrate, the higher the probability that the memories are much more difficult to rid of.

People have different views of migration. Some are tempted to look at it as an escape, to see it as that one and only chance to get away from a past life that is not so good and worth forgetting. Why not? Everybody deserves a chance to start a new life.

On the other hand, you might also have it so good that you do not want to leave at all. But what happens sometimes is that even if you are in the middle of good things, some bad things might still be happening, and interpret those bad things as reasons for you to leave.

Suddenly, the boss is too bossy, co-workers are unkind, traffic is stressful, projects are not challenging, those guys at the meeting are too obnoxious. Everything sucks and you want out. Then, you say to yourself, "Good thing, I am leaving soon."

But have you ever thought of that as plain and simple jitters? Anxiety, fear of leaving. Pretty soon, you'd come to terms with everything. You would and should realize that nobody wants to leave with a heavy heart. Nobody wants to leave with ill feelings. No one would want to be completely cut off from his or her past.

Whether by choice or by circumstance, it will not be the wisest thing to cut yourself off from these people. You will need them, even if only to hasten your emotional stability in a new place, by being able to connect or stay connected. Also, if you were able to create a good employment or professional record, the more important it becomes that you stay in good relationship with former colleagues, bosses or employers.

If you had come to another country without knowing anybody as references, most probably you will need to give the name of your past or immediate supervisor as well as friends and colleagues in the industry. My first serious job in Canada started from an email introduction from a good friend's client-friend from my own country.

This includes even best friends or classmates who got to the top rank much ahead of you whom you were tempted to envy but did not. Those relatives or related extensions are in position or in a position to drop nice words for you. You may not like them through and through, but believe me, you will need them.

1. *Make sure you left in good standing with most everyone.*
2. *Take advantage of technology to stay connected to them.*
3. *You will need them for sure, either as job reference or simply to help root you in your new country to keep going there.*

1.5   **Can You Forget the Good Times, Even if it Hurts?**

DON'T ALLOW THE GOOD TIMES IN YOUR PAST WEIGH YOU DOWN SO THAT YOU ARE IMMOBILIZED TO MOVE FORWARD. PULL THEM IN OR OUT OF YOUR MEMORY TO INSPIRE YOU THAT YOU CAN CREATE NEW GOOD TIMES, WHEREVER YOU MAY BE.

Depending on how old you are and how great your professional life was or how intense the relationships you had formed, moving on will be either easy or surprisingly difficult.

Parents worry about the kids when moving. Oh well, parents do that all the time. But they always say, children are the easiest to adjust. But have we ever bothered to explain that to ourselves? But now you begin to realize that the reason is simple: they have less experiences in life, less baggage to weigh them down, and less concerns to worry about.

The later in life you decide to go, the heavier the decision will be because by then you will have accumulated so much. That seems arithmetical. But the emotional content of that, we can never be able to measure. The happier you are in your past life, the more difficult it is to leave it behind you. The closer your family ties, the heavier the feeling when you need to go alone.

So what do you do? I am pretty sure somebody will protest if I suggest "Forget the good times." I recall a time when I made a confession to a priest, and I had to tell the priest that one of the sins that bothered me was, "I can forgive, but I cannot forget the wrong done to me."

The father-confessor very lovingly counselled that, as a rational being, we may never be able to forget a lot of things that happen in our lives, especially those that have the strongest impact on us, like those that hurt us the most. On the other hand, he said, man is so weak that forgiving somebody who had hurt us requires that we summon enough courage to do so. It should be a personal decision. We need to decide to forgive. It starts with a decision, and the healing will follow. With healing comes forgetting the pain that came with the hurt. Forgetting will never become complete because the experience of pain will cross your mind every now and then. But with healing, you will come to realize that the memory is reduced to being simply cognitive (meaning, confined to the mind), and no longer pierces your heart.

So what about the good times? Should I forget them like they were hurtful experiences, too? I should say the process is almost the same, but with a little bit of twist. Hurt or no hurt, we use the same rational processes.

Forgetting the good times is a decision. The forgetting part may also be cognitive, but so unlike the bad times, you may want to remember the feeling or allow the good feeling to stay. But even if you have decided to forget, the feeling does not die and becomes something you can pull out conveniently when you need it or when you want to.

1. *The sooner in your life you have the option to go, do it. Then the memories will be fewer.*
2. *Forgetting the good times is a decision. But as a rational being, it is not possible to forget the past completely.*
3. *That's just right the way it is, because you might want to pull those memories in and out of your thoughts whenever you need to be inspired in your new life or new job.*

9

CHAPTER 2   CAREFULLY PLAN THE LIFE AHEAD

2.1   How Do You Really Prepare Yourself?

> PREPPING UP YOURSELF FOR MIGRATION IS SOMETHING YOU OWE TO YOURSELF. USE THE WAITING PERIOD FOR APPROVAL TO MAKE AN INFORMED AND RATIONAL DECISION.

Many times, things that come our way are not necessarily those that we had hoped for or prepared for.

Where I once was and where I am now is not something I had ever dreamed of. While in school, I was too concerned with being able to maintain good grades that I did not have time to dream. Or maybe I was dreaming as I maintained that free schooling. I was obsessed with the fear that if I did not go to college, I'd be a nobody. That is not always true, of course.

Perhaps my only real dream was to have my own family. At age two, my only sister and I had been given away separately to relatives. At age nineteen, I was already starting a family, and I did not have any more dreams than that. But because I was used to working hard, my professional life went smoothly, bringing me up the ladder of success, not quite quickly, but steadily up nonetheless.

There are no accidents in life. Just as I was getting settled to a company that I thought could very well take care of me through my useful years, something came knocking. This. The chance to migrate.

I did not dream then. Why would I dream now? I never dreamt to go abroad and seek the proverbial greener pasture. Woe to me, I did not even know that one could go abroad without any relative petitioning for him. But we never know how our whole life can be preparation for something we may not even have aspired for.

I believed that the education I was obsessed with and the profession that I got into afterward were my only sure-fire investments, including the people that I had met along the way. However, these people were the key factors that prepared me for what was to come.

Even still, going abroad is a tough, emotional decision. Nothing actually prepares you for it.

And deciding to leave for good is an action that does not happen overnight. But there is plenty of time to decide to be ready. For example, on average, approval of migration to Canada under the skilled professional category took 4-6 years during my time. That is so much time to get prepared.

Preparing oneself is very important because your frame of mind, disposition and strength of character will cue the direction towards which everyone will be heading for or will be adapting to. Notwithstanding the fact that I had not dreamt to live abroad, once the opportunity was clear, my mind settled into the idea that this was real. Your mind should do the same.

Begin by imagining what life could be like abroad. There is so much that you might have heard or read about. You have to internalize these conceptions of life abroad, slowly but surely. Go through a role play in your mind. Is it a role you want to be in? Or is it a role you think you can play well? Think of things that you could do that you've never done before. Imagine the chance to have a new life, perhaps quieter, but more stable, one that may be uncertain, but promising.

1. **Use the waiting period as a time to learn about the country you are going to.**

2. Use your imagination a lot. Role play and keep updated.
3. How prepared you are may decide the difference on how fast
   you can land in that job you wanted.

2.2   What About Your Family?

> PREPARING YOUR FAMILY FOR MIGRATION IS NO MEAN
> TASK. IT TAKES PERSEVERANCE AND A CONSISTENT
> RECORD THAT THEY CAN TRUST YOUR DECISION. THE
> HAPPIER EVERYONE IS, THE EASIER YOU CAN BEAR THE
> BURDEN OF JOB HUNTING.

The principle is simple: the bigger the family, the more complicated any planning or preparation will be. Prepping up yourself is just that, yourself. Once you have decided to make the move, your personal pre-planning almost happens naturally. But family is different.

It starts as soon as you break the news that you have decided to move abroad. Not to visit, not for pleasure, not even for a temporary work contract, but for good. It is like changing the course or direction of the ship that you are all sailing on. This sounds totalitarian. Going through a full family consultation is even more difficult and complicated, but do it the way it works for your family.

To uproot oneself, much less a whole family, is major, really major. Depending on the size of the family, and the ages of the children to be uprooted, the harder things can get. But how do you break the news? How do you really plan a family for a major decision like this?

Cut to the chase. If the children are minor, whether small minors or big minors, it is always good to give it to them straight. You are all leaving and this is best situation for everyone as far as you have thought things out. Only a twist of fate, like an unlikely winning in the lotto jackpot, could possibly change that.

Most likely, the big minors will want to say something. Hear them out. But since they are minor, you are still the decision-maker. Unless any objection is violent, the family has to be together in this because that is the reason it is called a family.

After the decision has been announced, start introducing the adoptive country to the family. I remember putting up bond-sized posters around the house telling bits and pieces of Canada—its origin, provinces, government, weather, languages, economy, etc.

I came home with news clippings that told of good news about the country we were moving to. Tell the family good stories, success stories, happy endings. Of course, there are also not-so-good stories, and you will need to tell those, too. But as part of the planning, you need to stay positive.

Remind them how technology allows people to connect so easily nowadays. There are cell phones, VOIP, the Internet, the chat room, social media networks. Most of these are at virtually no extra cost at all, except for the high speed connection which you will need to get and the PC or the laptop which you most possibly already have.

Much of the food that they enjoy eating back home can be cooked or found in stores abroad, too. I myself was amazed at how my favourite spices and ingredients are in real Canadian groceries. Multi-cultural stores are conveniently located all over. And you might be surprised to discover that the well-loved local delicacy might even taste better than what is available in your home country.

Schools are well-funded by the government. Even private schools are not necessarily expensive if you take an effort to donate your time as a school volunteer. In this time and age, people have spread themselves far and wide, and the kids are likely to have someone from your own country as classmates, teachers, school staff or administrators. A good education is waiting for them.

Best of all, a family is a family. As long as the family sticks together, the easier it is to hurdle any challenges. The mother or the father or whoever is head of the family owes it to their children to make good decisions. Their children should have faith in that just as they have faith in the Supreme Being.

1. ***Make family a part of your conscious planning, especially if they are going with you.***
2. ***Keeping them realistically informed is key.***
3. ***A family united in a decision makes everybody's job hunting easier.***

2.3   Should Friends Know Your Plan?

THERE IS NO HARD AND FAST RULE ON THE EXTENT YOU WANT TO INVOLVE YOUR FRIENDS IN YOUR PLAN. BUT WITH TRUE FRIENDS AS YOUR WEALTH, THEY WILL SURELY BE ABLE MAKE YOUR NEW LIFE EASIER.

For those who were not born with the proverbial spoon in their mouths, wealth can be translated in other dimensions. Having many friends is one of these.

You probably have heard this saying—*tell me who your friends are and I will tell you who you are*. True? This saying is not that you should judge and categorize, but it is often told to us by our elders as a warning. If friends are to be your only wealth, they need to be the kind that will support you, bring the best in you as a person, and lead you to achieve. True friends are hard to find because they are as invisible as the wind. You do not see them, but they are always there. And the truer the friendships, the heavier it becomes to have to decide to leave or be far away for them. But the truer the friends, the happier they'd be for your big decisions. The more unselfish they are, the more they'll let go.

There are friends you'd leave behind, but what about the long-lost friends you'll be coming home to, the ones who will welcome you in the new country you are embracing? Are you sure you'll be welcomed unreservedly?

Even with technology, there are reasons that you could drift apart from friends. Sometimes it just happens, sometimes it just have to happen because that is how your own circumstances can best be handled. But a true friend will always welcome you back, shortcomings notwithstanding. But if you want to be able to do it right, remember what I told you earlier about not burning bridges. You will never know when you're going to need to cross that bridge again. Continue the line of communication with your friends. It is difficult to re-establish and repair any damage to friendship. And even if repair is possible, the scar that will remain will always remind you of your past indiscretions or plain thoughtlessness.

True friends will always be true friends regardless. They will be there to support you. But this you must remember—friends will only support you in a certain way and to a certain extent. It is good that what they can do for you, what you want them to do, or what they want to do for you, is clear to you.

Do not expect too much. Do not think they will have all the solution you need as you adjust to a new life or search for a job. Your friends may be willing to help, but much of the work will still be in your hands.

You need all the help you can get. Your friends can be a source of information, of contacts, referrals, or plain advice. Keep asking for information here and there. Do not hesitate. Do not be ashamed. I always tell my children that if you do not steal from anyone or short-change anybody, there's nothing to be ashamed of.

1. *It is best that your true friends know about your plans. You may need them.*
2. *The truer your friends, the easier for you to start moving forward, knowing they will be there anytime.*
3. *Starting a new life and looking for a new job still relies much on the work of your own hands, but true friends will be a great source of strength.*

2.4   What Do You Want to Be When You Get There?

> NEEDING TO PLAN FOR A CAREER, WHETHER FOR A
> CONTINUATION OF WHAT YOU HAD OR STARTING A NEW
> ONE, IS INEVITABLE. WHATEVER YOUR DREAM JOB IS,
> CONSIDER THIS: IF YOU CAN IMAGINE IT, YOU CAN DREAM
> IT. IF YOU CAN DREAM IT, YOU CAN ACHIEVE IT.

What do you want to be when you grow up? How many of us were asked this classic question when we were small kids?

On your migration, it might not be the right question to ask. However, the question can simply be rephrased, to wit: What do you want to be when you get there?

When I was saying goodbye to friends, I told them that even if family was my reason for leaving, I did not want to blame family for not being able to succeed at anything or get depressed for not being able to do anything useful. I was able then to enumerate at least five items in my personal agenda.

I could continue my career in marketing communications, redirect my talent in broadcasting, become rich as a real estate agent, grow old gracefully in the academe as a teacher, or simply write a book.

The more, the merrier? Perhaps, but not necessarily so. Your options can be as many as you can imagine. But when you get here, you will realize that those options may even multiply. And the danger is, you may begin to doubt what it is you really want.

Migrate with at least one burning desire in your heart. That desire may or may not be so big. But as I always say, it has to be CLEAR to you. It may not be a specific job or new career path, but it has to be imaginable. As they say, if you can imagine it, you can achieve it.

It is not surprising if what you may have in mind is a path that is entirely different from the job you do back home. This won't matter as long as you decide to pursue this new path as quickly as you can. This is because if it is going to be entirely new, the learning curve will be longer and investments of time, effort, and even money will be more.

Regardless of the level of position you had back home or the career success you enjoyed there, migration affords you to very conveniently switch careers, and not mind having to start from the ranks all over again.

Your planning for yourself and your own career path should welcome that possibility.

Regardless of age, starting all over again can be amazingly graceful when you hardly know people. You should not be afraid of being degraded, mocked, or looked down upon.

Just be yourself. Work at it. If your need will be too immediate because there are no savings to draw from and there are dependents to feed, plan for that, too. Plan in such a way that you will not mind starting out much, much lower in rank or type of work.

1. *Plan for a career path, whether for something you used to do or a new one.*
2. *If you are taking an entirely new career direction, waste no time working for it, because investments of time, effort and personal money may be higher.*
3. *The happy news is, regardless of age or previous level or education or profession, it can be amazingly graceful to start anew in another country.*

2.5   Have You Done Your Research?

DO YOUR HOMEWORK. ONLY AN INFORMED DECISION WILL MAKE IT EASY FOR YOU TO WHEEL YOUR FORTUNE TOWARDS THE LIFE YOU DREAMED OF.

How much do you know about the country you are moving to?

What made you decide to choose one country from another? Why Canada? Why not Australia? New Zealand? Or other countries? What is it about this or that country that attracted you? Or you have never even thought about asking yourself these questions?

I do not want to think that majority of us are caught in a situation where we will just take off to the first country that will take us. We are not necessarily compelled to jump into a boat because we are refugees or political asylum seekers.

That being said, we have time and the resources to check out what we are going into. Doing that has never been easier with the Internet and all the progress of technology. If you did not do that when you left, do it now.

Where is this place on the map? Who inhabits it? Who rules it? What is the culture? How big is it? How cold is it there? How many people populate it? How do people live?

If there is one thing really necessary, study its economic profile because you are not going there for a vacation, you are going there to build a life. You will need a job, a source of livelihood.

Which industries thrive? Which ones are developing fast? What skills are they looking for? Do you have those skills? Are the people there prosperous or are they poor? Are they complaining or are they happy?

What can the government promise me if I make enough money for them to be able to collect taxes from me? How will my children benefit? How will my old age and my medical needs be provided for?

In what part of this country should I settle? Which province can offer me greater opportunities? Which one needs me and my skills?

I do not know anybody from this country. How do I socialize and network? Or if I have distant relatives or long-lost friends there somewhere, how do I connect or re-connect with them?

To my mind, it will be your own fault if you come here and realize you know nothing. It is not like you were led here by somebody who blindfolded you. You have all the freedom and the chance in the world to know as much as possible about the place. There is not a news blackout or some such thing preventing you from knowing the harsh realities of being able to survive abroad.

Coming is a personal decision. Any decision-making must be an informed one. It was not like you were made to enter your marriage with a shotgun to your head.

1. *Learn as much about the country you want to migrate to.*
2. *Because you are coming in to look for a job, check out the state of economy.*
3. *Your chances of succeeding are higher if you are well aware of the opportunities that your adapted country presents.*

CHAPTER 3   DO YOU HAVE THE RIGHT ATTITUDE?

3.1   Are You Decisive?

THERE IS NO CUT-OUT FORMULA ON HOW TO MAKE A FINAL DECISION. IF YOU HAVE THE MONEY, THE REASON IS COMPELLING, YOU HAVE DONE YOUR RESEARCH, AND YOU FEEL GOOD ABOUT IT, THEN YOU JUST KNOW.

I know at least three people who have asked me ten years ago how to migrate. True to form, I patiently explained the process, printed the necessary forms, walked them through the appropriate website. Today, they are still back home figuring out how to migrate.

It takes a decision, a firm decision. If the matter is not simple, then it may have to take a little bit of time to make the final decision, but you will still have to make one. If you cannot do that, then something is not clear that needs to be, or there was really no intention to make a decision in the first place.

Just for an example, it took me only two weeks to decide whether or not to go, then another six weeks to secure all the documents required for the skilled professional category. Then I chose a date, my birth date, on which I would not forget to file my application, so that I would know when my filing anniversary fell every year of waiting.

I should like to understand people who may not find it easy to decide on a big matter like packing up and leaving your country for good. I have two things to discuss here.

First, if the money you will spend for filing the application is spare money or something you really have saved up for this purpose, then file it as soon as you can. Let years pass you by with your application efficiently counting the time for you. It takes an average of three to four years before applications can be approved; five to six years for some, and in rare cases, only one to two years, which might be a little bit too soon for many. Thus, there is plenty of time to think things over. Consider whatever you pay as an investment that may pay off for you, or money you would spend or depreciate some other way anyway. But the best thing is that time is flying on your side.

Second, leaving is really not a joke, but a very major decision. But to me, no one ever leaves for good. *Country will always stay there in your heart, in your whole being.* Country will always be there to welcome you back and to enjoy for a visit. Friends will always be there, if you have chosen them well. You cannot choose relatives, but they will also be there when you visit.

How do you make the final decision? I cannot give you a formula. If you have the money, if the reason is compelling, if you had done your research, if you feel good about it, you just know. It is just in you. Even if you do not have the money now but have a way of raising it when you get an approval, then the decision should come along.

How a person makes decisions—how fast or how firm—speaks of how he has made out in his lifetime and how he wants to see his future. Sometimes, the person just needs a little push or encouragement. In the absence of people who will do that for you, make sure you are well informed. An informed decision is a good decision. And only you can make it for yourself.

1. *Making good decisions does not happen overnight, nor does it have a cut formula.*
2. *Assuming you meet requirements, it is important to be fully aware or informed.*
3. *Next to a decision is the action. Do it as soon as possible so that time passes by working for you.*

3.2   Are You Positive?

> REMEMBER, WHEN EVERYTHING SEEMS UNREACHABLE FOR NOW, ONLY YOUR POSITIVE ATTITUDE CAN MAKE YOU HOLD ON AND REACH OUT FOR THAT SOMETHING.

With the world around you contributing to your own set of anxieties, it seems so much easier to be unhappy, discouraged, or passive. You may even be in a situation where no matter how hard you work, the returns do not improve and you do not become happier or richer. Maybe you cannot even figure out what could dramatically change your situation.

How difficult can being positive be? Is it a choice or is it something you are born with? Are there really negative people vs. positive people? Are there really people who are pessimists vs. those that are optimists?

I caught a boob tube one-liner plug, *"Our deepest fear is our potential for inadequacies."* There will always be that gnawing fear in our hearts that daily provisions will not be enough, that our efforts will not pay off, that our energy may run out, that our capacity to keep trying may be gone faster that we could ever imagine.

Have you ever wondered why man is born naked? Well, other than the physiological reasons, it tells us that we are born into this world with nothing except our being. At first, everything has to be provided to us. Later, we provide for ourselves. Pretty soon, we provide for others, too—family, loved ones, friends, and even to people we do not even know.

It is that possibility of not being able to provide anymore or receive provisions that discourages or threatens us and destabilizes our sense of confidence. And when you are not confident, it is difficult, and perhaps impossible, to stay positive.

The key to staying positive is being able to preserve your self-esteem. When you are in a new place with fewer friends or relatives, or none at all, it is quite a challenge to hold on to that level of confidence from where you had taken off. And I must say, this is worst for those who had successful careers as skilled professionals in their own country.

Of course you hear that a strong support system is important. But some of us may not have that. You may only have yourself and this new world around you. So what do you do?

Gather your little victories every single day. Find things to do, and find happiness in doing them. And you need to say that aloud to yourself. It could be anything at all. It could be assembling IKEA furniture, cooking a meal straight off of an internet recipe, being able to find the right direction from Google map, getting the best bargains, or moving to a new, more comfortable apartment.

You may not always be adequate but you can certainly choose to be happy. You can choose to trust yourself, and have faith that when you are down, there is no other way to go but up.

1. **The key to staying positive is being able to preserve your self-esteem.**
2. **Gather triumphs every day. Find things to do and find happiness in doing them.**
3. **The positive attitude will be your strongest weapon in claiming your stake in this new place.**

3.3   Can You Look Forward?

> IF EXCELLENCE IS A WAY OF LIFE WITH YOU, IT WILL SHINE THROUGH SO THAT LOOKING FORWARD AND MOVING ON WILL NEVER BE IMPOSSIBLE.

Allow me to differentiate between being positive and being forward-looking. Although both traits imply that we should not sulk, being positive presents a state of mind, a happy disposition. To me, to be forward-looking is to make a decision to take a certain direction or path into the future and not to go back to where you had come from regardless of whether it was the better place to be.

I must admit, in the beginning, when it was very difficult, for as simple a reason as the weather getting too cold for comfort—there was always the temptation to run back to the life I left behind. I chided myself for the masochism. Why move to a wooden bed when you are sleeping on the softest mattress?

I may not have had the best life in my home country, but it was good. I'm pretty sure that many of those who have migrated can say the same of theirs. Thus, to the barest minds, it is unthinkable to leave your good life and move to one that is full of uncertainty.

When you had this good life, is it easy to look forward to better things ahead? Probably—it is a hope, the hope to continue doing well. But if it is not so good and is not turning well as easily as we had thought it should, isn't being forward-looking even easier? That is the best time when being forward-looking becomes almost inevitable.

As mentioned before, the past good times must inspire you; looking back must trigger in you the desire to do just as well, if not better. Or maybe, it must trigger the thought that you once had it good in your life, and any more good that comes must be a bonus.

When you look forward, it is because you have made a decision to move on. You have decided that life needs to go on and that the future is the best place to move into. Moving on also implies a lot of hope and confidence not only in your ability to stay afloat, but also confidence in the opportunities that your circumstances present to you.

Best of all, look forward because it is the best thing to do. It is the best direction you can take. There is no basis for living in your past and dwelling on old glories.

Do not be afraid that you cannot do it again, that you cannot be good again. *If you are good, you are good, no matter the time, the circumstances, and the people around you.* The real you and your excellence will shine through because there can only be you, and this you will sooner or later be discovered or reflected in everything you do.

1. *To look forward is to decide to move into the direction of the future.*
2. *To do that, you have to trust that your good works will follow you everywhere.*
3. *When you find that first job, all that is past will help you look forward to a next successful chapter in your life.*

3.4   Can You be Humble?

> A PERSON WHO IS NOT WHOLE HIMSELF CAN NEVER BE HUMBLE. IT TAKES A STRONG, COURAGEOUS AND STABLE PERSON TO ADMIT TO HIS OWN WEAKNESSES AND BOUNCE BACK WITH TWO FEET FIRMLY GROUNDED.

I have always been a white-collar person. My jobs had always involved my ability to think, analyze and strategize, and I have never been tested for my agility or physical endurance.

In Canada, when I had a lot of free time in my hands, I took on a volunteer job as a "doorman" for a private school. Really easy, right? Just make sure you unlock the door where the kids will enter and let them in. Really easy? Let me say that again. Some co-parents complained about me for not doing my job well because I failed to assist their kids when coming in to enter.

I had to argue that I use my discretion as to which kids I should assist or open the door for, and only did so for the small ones and those with a lot of bags. I said that these kids needed to learn to be independent and be able to open the door by themselves. Apparently, that was not acceptable to everybody. These parents said I overestimated some kids, and so they were mad.

That issue was resolved, of course. But it was not easy going back to that door the following duty day knowing those parents would be there watching my every move. I had three options: I could pay somebody else to do my job for me, I could tell the school that I was giving up the discount that comes with the volunteer work, or I could go back next time to try again and do better. What do you think did I do?

I was a top-ranking bank officer from where I came from, multi-awarded for the excellent work that I had always delivered and, most of all, respected for my hard work and dedication to my craft. Yet, I could not be a good "doorman"? How do you think I felt?

I felt humiliated, of course. I was bruised. My ego had been deflated. I was tempted to sulk in self-pity. I wanted to cry and run away. I could not even tell the story to my own kids. I was afraid that they'd think less of me. The mother who they have always known for her high achievements could not do her doorman job well.

But I decided to face up to it. I went back and did better and better each time.

I remember having always advised our clerks and messengers in the office that, when we all die and face our judgment, we will not be distinguished by the position or title we held on earth. The only question that will be put before us is: How well did you perform each task that was assigned to you? And that could well be the same measure that will be used to gather your rewards Up There.

It takes a lot of humility to be reduced to a minor role or job. But it takes more humility to be allowed to be corrected so you can perform that role well. Well, some may say it is almost always so natural to be humble in a small role. But what about those in big roles? How can you be humble in a big role?

Some of you can be lucky and be able to get into a job that is nearly equivalent to your former job. It can be a good start to recognize that being in a new place or new environment requires a lot of learning and submission to others there ahead of you or who know better than you. It is most rewarding to be thought of as a person who had the humility to accept corrections and welcome others' ideas and guidance.

Pray that you don't learn the greatest lesson in humility the hard way, because you may not like it at all.

1. *Being in a new place, it is possible to find yourself not knowing how to do things well.*
2. *There is no difference between doing a minor or a big role. You have to do well in either.*
3. *Humility, a lot of humility, will enable you to gather your lessons better and faster.*

3.5 **Are you Grateful?**

> IF YOU CANNOT BE GRATEFUL FOR SMALL THINGS, HOW CAN YOU EXPECT TO BE WORTHY OF BIGGER THINGS? GRATEFULNESS PREPARES YOU TO RECEIVE GREAT THINGS ACTUALLY.

You probably have heard it before, *"Many are called but only few are chosen."*

If you had come from an underdeveloped or a developing country, you probably will never know how many of your own countrymen look up to you, some with pride, some with envy, that you had this much-coveted chance to move to a more progressive country and start to carve a brighter future.

Yet coming, here, sometimes only we know how difficult starting a new life can be, much more hoping for a better life. Perhaps, we choose to keep mum because we want to make a go of it really, or because we are afraid people will judge us for having made a mistake. This difficulty or seeming difficulty practically prevents us from seeing the good side of what we have. It may actually threaten to consume us.

But before it consumes us in any way, let's rewind. Take a few steps back to try to remember back to one or several points in your life when you had fervently wished for this to happen, or how hard you had tried to focus your efforts, your energies, or perhaps your lifetime savings just so you could leave. So, how could it be wrong? How can you not be so grateful for your new opportunities?

Gratefulness need not be a reactive behaviour or attitude, only in response to something you have already received. Of course, you can be thankful that you made it here. But now what?

I want you to think of gratefulness as being a prayer, like a mantra that you sing to yourself every day for every little victory already won and, most especially, for those still to come, a job, a new job, a good job coming.

If anything at all, gratefulness is a happy, positive feeling. You do not want to be angry, bitter, depressed and unhappy. Rather, you should choose to be grateful now and look to the better days ahead instead of the possible gloomy days.

Yesterday is past, tomorrow is not yet here, so today is all you have. So, why be unhappy today when you can choose to be happy and grateful? I remember when my oldest son was just learning how to drive, I would tell him about the men who drive older cars like they own the road. "See that guy? He'll never get a nicer, newer car later in his life. You know why? Because he cannot even drive an old one right."

1. *Gratefulness is a happy, positive feeling. Choose it.*
2. *Sing gratefulness to your soul like a mantra. Anticipate with happiness in your heart that the right job will come in perfect time.*
3. *Always remember that, if you cannot learn to be grateful for small things, greater things will not have a place in your life.*

CHAPTER 4   LET US TALK ABOUT MONEY MATTERS

4.1   How Much Money Do You Need?

> WHEREVER YOU ARE, THE REALITY IS THAT YOU ALWAYS NEED TO INVEST IN YOUR FUTURE. MIGRATING IS BETTER CONSIDERED AS AN INVESTMENT RATHER THAN AS A GAMBLE.

I had a helper back home who, because of poverty, was not able to go to school as a kid. She may not have been able to read or write, but she could surely count her money accurately. After all, as the wife of a dictator once said, "You are not rich if you can count your money. Me, I am rich because I do not know how much money I have."

The desire to migrate is not a simple dream. It is expensive. It is not as easy as lining up for a job, getting the interview and expecting to earn a decent living for that job. In fact, it can be the opposite. When you migrate, you start putting in your own money first, spend that to sustain yourself, and then hope to earn a living later when you get a job and save your money back.

It is like each new immigrant has to invest his own money first for a future. I have read some blogs and went over some forum posts whose authors cannot accept that reality, expressing their own frustration, sometimes anger. They say that they have been lured, only to find out that it will not be easy to get that first pay check.

But nobody can ever force anyone to a decision as big as migrating, or uprooting oneself or leaving country for good. The terms of engagement are pretty clear and fully laid out before our very own eyes. The decision to meet the financial requirements of the migration process is a free choice.

To some, it could be the lifetime savings, the retirement money, house and lot sold, an inheritance advanced, or blue chip stocks monetized. Whatever the source of your funding to migrate, the decision must have been conscious and your senses in control when it was made.

Thus, it can be said that under the skilled professional category, Canada gets the cream of the crop. The educated, mostly middle class, the highly-motivated, strongly driven: That is the kind of stuff that skilled immigrant professionals are made of.

Yet, coming and starting all over again is such a challenge to the pocket. Whether you are starting with the minimum required money, or bringing in more, you are bound to spend it and pray that you money does not run out before you get that first job.

This aspect increases the worries, the anxieties, and perhaps the regrets, especially for those bringing in a whole family. The tension may even impact your relationships, with the grown-up children or spouse who may not be prepared, may not fully understand, and may not be as supportive.

1. *Migrating will cost you money.*
2. *It is better to think of this money as your investment for everyone in your family.*
3. *Be prepared for the challenge that the money may run out fast and that first pay check may come only in the nick of time.*

4.2   Do You Have Any Financial Baggage?

YOU WILL NEVER KNOW WHEN YOU CAN GET THAT FIRST JOB, SO REDUCE THE FINANCIAL BURDEN BY STRIVING TO START ON A CLEAN SLATE. BREAK FREE FROM DEBTS.

Wherever you are, in whatever stage of struggle you are in, there will always be a desire deep, deep down inside to come out clean of debts or financial obligation.

I am sorry to say that, no matter how hard companies try to prettify credit card usage and maintenance, many people still ruin their lives by overextending their borrowings. It's an oft-repeated cry for help— people wanting to be free from credit cards or debts, in general.

But to some, that is only the tip of the iceberg. While immigrant hopefuls are always reminded not to declare borrowed money in order to meet financial requirements, some still do so. Although it should be noted that meeting such requirement is not necessarily the reason or only reason some have gotten into debts. The reason is the same as why they want to leave—economic issues that could really be personal or societal. The financial problem had been there and so the decision to seek greener pasture.

It is most ideal to start a new life on a clean slate. It will not be good to be haunted by your financial indiscretions in the past, much less hunted by creditors.

Unless you have extra funds, it will be difficult to achieve freedom from debt. But you should try, and try hard. As soon as you have reckoned with all the necessary expenses in connection with your leaving, including the required show money, do not have second thoughts about cleaning up all your financial obligations. Start with those that charge interest the highest. Hopefully, no one is a victim of freelance loan sharks that charge exorbitant rates. My grandmother used to say that loan sharks are being burned in hell while still alive due to their heartless entrepreneurship.

Abroad, chances are, the first bank you will meet will offer you a credit card. You should get one, not only because you need it to build up your credit history, but also because you are now in a plastic card society. However, be wise in choosing the type of credit card to use. Choose the one that even pays you or rewards you for using it.

Once you are settled in, it is not surprising to discover how fast and easy those credit cards and high finance instruments are to come by. And as you are able to build up your reputation, you will be bombarded with offers for credit cards, personal loans, and all types of financial accommodations. This, matched with sales here and there, zero interest plans, and deferred payment offers.

With that, you are surely on your way to the same financial problems. So, watch out or you will soon find yourself in the same personal economic quagmire as you were before you migrated.

Cut clean, and cut cleanly. Coming to a new country, start clean. Do not allow any temptation to go back to the old debt-ridden life.

1. ***If you can, rid yourself of all debts.***
2. ***Start with ridding yourself of those that charge interest highest.***
3. ***Looking for your first job will be rendered less burdensome if you do not have financial ghosts.***

4.3   Can You Save Up?

SAVING UP IS A UNIVERSAL VIRTUE. YOU WILL NEED LOTS OF SAVINGS WHEN YOU GO, AS THEY WILL BE ALL YOU CAN SPEND WHILE YOU ARE STILL LOOKING FOR A JOB.

Leaving or not leaving, saving up is a must. It is universal, timeless virtue. People do it. And those who can't do it for now, always have it at the back of their minds.

People complain of not earning enough to be able to set aside money for savings. The money coming in will be just enough to meet monthly expenses. Thus, no matter how earnestly you want or decide to save, you cannot.

Not even the firmest decision can make one decide to save up if he does not have a plan, a wish, a desire, an ambition. You save for something you look forward to, for something you want to happen. My old aunt was right when she admonished me, "When you save, do not do it because you want emergency money for hospital bills or funeral expenses. Do it for a positive reason." If the reason is good, then saving up becomes heart-warming and a source of hope.

Migration, as we said, is a big step. But it does not happen overnight. It is as if one is given ample time to prepare well, psychologically and financially.

In the financial services sector, we always remind our clients that saving money does not mean just depositing cold cash in the bank on a regular basis. Insurance, pension plans, real estate, stocks, jewellery all count as savings. Anything that appreciates in value and you can monetize when you need it. A small townhouse that I bought easily amounted to the needed show money when we had to land. Even the cars that we had owned translated to money that we could bring to help us tide over.

Although some of your accumulations will actually depreciate in value, as long as they can be monetized easily, they should help raise money. I remember having held at least three garage sales in the period of time we were waiting for an approval.

Whatever amount of cash you have been able to raise, through savings and selling here and there, keep in mind to try to service some, if not all of your loans, starting, as I said, with the ones with the highest interest rates.

In Canada, I was amazed to realize how almost accurate the amount of show money they computed and required was in lasting until I found a job. I figure you should have enough for six months to a year, depending how big is the family and how tightly you hold on to your wallet.
Once you get to your new country, it is all spend, spend, spend...until you get that first job. So while you are not there yet, save, save, save. You are going to need every penny you can save, keep, or bring with you later.

While you will probably have some friends and relatives around you in your new country, you will not want to be borrowing and creating a reputation as a borrower early on. You will also not want to go back to the old debt-ridden life, I am sure.

You should have a computation of the exact figure of how much money you bring with you.   For your peace of mind, why not try to save up just that exact amount as soon as you start working or at least when you start recovering from the initial expenses? It should be fun and, well, reassuring.

1. *You will need to save up or raise money when you leave.*
2. *Save up while you can or sell out accumulations which you cannot bring or will not want to bring with you.*
3. *Once you start working, it might be good to start recovering saved-up money spent by saving up again.*

4.4   Can You Stick to the Right Expenses?

YOU MAY NEED TO GO BACK TO THE BASICS WHEN YOU'RE LIVING ON THE SAVINGS YOU BROUGHT WITH YOU UNTIL THAT FIRST JOB COMES AROUND.

When you have a full, well-provided life, it could happen that your lifestyle no longer distinguishes between the basics and the excesses. This is simply because those little excesses have almost become like basics, things you cannot do without.

Speaking of basics, you will certainly go back to the basics when you start living on your savings. Whether it is by force of that circumstance or by choice, there is no escaping the fact that there will be expenses you will encounter for the first time, although they will be classified as basics.

For example, prospective immigrants from tropical countries are so afraid of the cold season. You will realize the only important thing is to be able to bundle up properly. Thus, what it takes or how much it will cost you to bundle up is one of those expenses that suddenly becomes necessary.

If you were not used to paying your own medical insurance, then that becomes another necessary expense. This can be temporary until you qualify for a 100% waiver, in which case that means you are either in the low-income bracket or have no income at all. Different provinces have their own health care programs, some are free from the first day you arrive. Unfortunately, it is not absolutely free in some.

A friend of mine advised that I get good accommodations, especially if I am bringing grown-up minors. The big kids have already formed opinions on some things, and for them to have a good first impression of your moving it is common sense to give them a decent, comfortable home. It is bad enough they are being uprooted; it is worse to have them live in a rundown dwelling when you can afford a better one.

However, your moving might also be a good chance for the kids to learn how to start life from scratch or live life all over again. Perhaps they never saw how you struggled to raise them when they were growing up. Now they will see how all of you will need to take baby steps once again, supporting one another to go through the next phase of your lives. This is the same case for singles migrating, who never knew how to start life from scratch when they were growing up because everything had been provided by their parents or guardians.

Expense-wise, it is good to know that eating good food or the right kind of food is not that burdensome. Even so, aiming for the ingredients and spices you knew back home can be very expensive. You will need to be practical and find substitutes, or switch to new recipes. That favourite food back home can be reserved for special occasions only.

1. *Determine expenses necessary to keep afloat without humiliating yourself.*
2. *After all, you cannot stay positive if you lose your self-esteem. Remember?*

3. *While scrimping may be temporary until you get a job, wise spending should be a permanent disposition and state of mind.*

4.5   Is It Gone Too Soon?

> WITHOUT THAT JOB, EROSION OF YOUR SAVINGS MAY BE INEVITABLE. BUT THIS DOES NOT HAVE TO EAT YOU UP AND LEAVE YOU WITHOUT SELF-ESTEEM AND DIGNITY.

Even if you keep your eyes wide, wide open, you will wake up one day to find out that the money you have brought with you will be gone.

This is scary. Really scary.

As I mentioned earlier, "Our deepest fear is our potential for inadequacies." This means our greatest fear is realizing that we cannot pay the rent and utilities, cannot service our loans or debts, or cannot afford to eat well.

The hope is really to not reach a point that you are down to zero. Have faith. Stay positive. But be sure to move quickly.

A friend, who had stayed many years in Canada as immigrant, put it simply, "You need to be proactive." The job will not fall on your lap or enter your inbox.

I know of someone who had a job just one week after she arrived. She walked around downtown, entered every shop that she thought she'd like to work in, and was able to get an interview after walking in. It was not necessarily the job to match her previous job, but it was enough to have something to tide her over and keep her bank withdrawals to a minimum.

A classmate in a workshop recalled her husband doing the same but was almost rejected because he was thought to be overqualified for the job in question. But he stated his case quite convincingly, specifically the fact that he had to feed his children, and he got the job.

A prospective employer confessed to me that out of hundreds of resumes emailed to him, only one person actually wrote a personalized cover letter and mentioned having visited his website. He then called that applicant and discussed that the job could very well be hers.

Since I have concluded that most skilled professionals coming as immigrants are well educated, have money and are highly motivated, I am pretty sure they can also be able to figure out by themselves when it is time to drop the gloves and roll with the punches.

With that, it might not have to come to a point when the money will be totally eroded before you are able to get that first job. Because if that happens, then taking on what they call a "survival job" becomes so literal you might not have much self-respect left in you. You will not like that, of course.

1. *No matter what you do, the money you bring with you will be gone if you do not get a job.*
2. *The key is to be able to act fast and prevent total monetary erosion.*
3. *Be careful when taking on a survival job. Keep your self-esteem intact so that you can stay positive.*

CHAPTER 5   DOES YOUR SUPPORT SYSTEM SUPPORT YOU?

5.1   What Can You Expect from Family?

> COMING AS A WHOLE FAMILY IS A CHANCE FOR EVERYONE TO GATHER VICTORIES TOGETHER, THIS TIME WITH EVERYBODY AWARE OF THEIR INDIVIDUAL ROLES AND NEED TO CONTRIBUTE.

Anybody who has experienced being away from home will agree that being able to leave with your family is better than having to leave alone. Those who had gone alone would attest to the fact that there is nothing like having your family beside you when you struggle and meet the challenges of starting a new life. That seems non-debatable.

But in fairness to those who have other opinions, some do choose to start the struggle alone. To some, it seems more practical to secure a job first and gain firm footing on new grounds before bringing family over. Perhaps the mindset is that you can better concentrate on a job hunt if there are no distractions or additional worries of having to break in the whole family at the same time. It can also be true that sometimes the family does not function as expected, and some members instead of being able to help, contribute to the problems.

I must admit I was tempted to start on my own and send for the rest of the family when that ideal job came along. This was not because the other family members would have been distractions, but rather because some mothers or fathers love their family so much that they do not want them to experience the hardship of starting all over again. There were also practical reasons, as the expenses would have been much less, considering the job search was just beginning.

However, as I believe I have mentioned before, bringing your whole family with you upon landing is a chance for everyone to start together and gather victories as a unit, this time with everybody aware of their own roles and what they can contribute.

It may be possible that none of your children have it in their conscious memory how hard you worked for them all your lives. Landing together is a way for everyone to live life all over again, but this time holding each other by the hand and winning together, laughing and crying together as a family.

There is no hard and fast rule on this debate. Of course, money is a big factor. If you have enough, then it is best to be together because you will be thinking about them and worrying about them anyway.

Whether the family lands and stays with you, or chooses to wait back home till you get a stable job, family will remain the best support system for a person starting life all over again.

1. *You could be lucky to have the choice whether to bring the whole family or send for them when you have the job.*
2. *There is no hard and fast rule, but family has always been defined as being together. Landing together is a way for everyone to live life all over again.*
3. *In general, family must fulfill its role as the best support system, not a deterrent to hastening the job search and desired stability in a new life.*

5.2   What About Relatives And Extended Families?

RELATIVES WILL INEVITABLY INFLUENCE SOME PARTS OF YOUR LIFE. YOU NEED TO BE PERCEPTIVE AND CIRCUMSPECT, BUT CONTINUE TO BE KIND ANYWAY.

There are certain nationalities whose definition of family is really a bit more extended. Even if you have been brought up having relatives or extended families around you and taught how to be respectful and grateful, blood or origin does not determine whether you have a heartfelt desire to be kind to everyone.

"Charity begins at home."

This is one best-loved quotable quotes that pounds your head every time you realize that you need to reach out and give. It seems wrong to be cited as a philanthropist if any of your relations is starving.

There is no generalization that needs to be made. Man is a rational being. He should be able to figure out by himself if there was an abuse or excess of support being asked or demanded of him. To us, watching from the sideline, we hate that and wish that the one being abused or burdened cry foul.

But it is true that there is such a word as masochism. It's not that this person wants to hurt himself, but that he is a person who takes pride in being solicited upon. Perhaps this is a person who wants to assert his authority over others by assuming the giver role. He could also be someone who is matriarchal or patriarchal in spirit. Being such, they therefore have to play the role as the one providing and leading. Why? Simply because he is what he is. He may complain sometimes, but it is a role that he still wants to play.

Relatives or not, people will influence some parts of your life and you need to recognize that yourself. While we hear sob stories about non-immediate families overburdening a migrant worker or immigrant with their own problems, we also hear of happy stories where the first people you can run to are these non-immediate family members.

There are some migrants or immigrants who purposely hide from or prevent closeness with these relatives for fear of being solicited upon, especially monetarily. We cannot blame some of them because we do not know their complete stories, like how they have been abused, defrauded, or misled by their own relatives.

But they can still form part of your support system. Going back to our question in this chapter, just make sure this support system also supports you. They may not have the material things you need to get by, but you should be able to turn to them for advice, a few errands, important information, or simply comfort—a listening ear and words of encouragement.

Again, whether you are dealing with relatives or non-relatives, it is important to be very perceptive and circumspect. Yet, there is always reason to be kind or extend kindness. I cannot teach you not to be. As a rational being, you certainly know what you should be or should not be doing.

1. *Relatives and extended families are born with you.*
2. *They will influence your life, but you can turn that towards something positive.*
3. *You can choose to be guarded while continuing to be kind.*

5.3　　　Can You Count on Your Friends?

SOMEONE ONCE SAID, TRUE FRIENDS ARE LIKE THE WIND. YOU DO NOT ALWAYS SEE THEM, BUT THEY ARE ALWAYS THERE.

Let me answer that question straight: If your friends cannot be any source of support, even just plain comfort, then I believe you have made the wrong friends. Why, even thieves help each other.

"Tell me who your friends are and I will tell you who you are."

Probably not a fair pronouncement, but I guess it has been formulated to remind us to be very careful in choosing our friends. One of the best achievements that anybody can be so proud about is to have been able to collect true friends. Not the fair-weather kind, but definitely those who will be there for you. Maybe not at any cost, but at least when you really need them or when you tell them that you need them.

When you phone a friend and tell her that you are so depressed and you need someone to talk to, and this friend says, "Ok, will call you back" and never does, what does that make of your friendship, assuming you know that there isn't any compelling reason that she couldn't call you back? Or perhaps, for the sake of argument, there is a valid reason not to be able to return the call, it will still be a letdown, right? And that could have still disappointed you.

A friend is a friend and if you know better, you are ready to understand. Trying to be the true friend yourself, you can choose to take the big sister or big brother role, forgive, forget and continue on with the friendship. But that could only go on for a while because eventually the relationship will take its toll on you.

Everything is all about choices.

How difficult your life is depends on the choices you have made, including the people you want to call your friends. At some point in time, you need to sit down to determine whether this is quite a one-sided friendship, and does not stand a chance to develop into a mutual proposition. Probably you will never want to do that upfront, but somehow time and distance will allow you to drift away.

When you find yourself thousands of miles away, you will realize that you do not even have to make an effort to distinguish the hay from the stack. You will soon know who are true and not true. Nevertheless, if you want to continue the friendship, just pretend you never noticed. As has been said, life is not about subtraction. You add or multiply whenever you can.

The other ticklish issue in friendship support that we can come across with is the answer to the question: Should friends be able to borrow from or lend money to each other?

Is money the source of all evil? That's not true, we are told, it is the love of money that is. But in any way you look at it, friends borrowing and lending each other money is a little bit uncomfortable. Perhaps this is the reason why a good, good friend of mine never waited for me to ask to borrow money. She always knew when I needed money. I never had to ask. This being the case, I have always tried to preserve that trust.

So, would you borrow or lend? It's bound to happen that money will come between some good friends. There is no right or wrong answer. The key is to be able to reach that level of friendship where money or the lack of it will never ruin anything. As for myself, I will never want any of my friendships to have to go or bruised because of money issues.

1. *A friend should be someone you can always turn to for support, regardless.*
2. *The level of support friends can expect from each other also depends on the extent the friendship has flourished or drifted apart.*
3. *Money, or the lack of it, should never be an issue that will ruin a friendship.*

5.4   Can You Count on Your Country-mates?

YOU WILL NEVER BE ALONE BECAUSE YOU'LL ALWAYS FIND SOMEBODY FROM THE SAME COUNTRY. YOU NEED ONLY TO ASK AND YOU SHALL FIND.

It might astound you, but in these global times, you will realize that you are not really, really alone. That is because wherever you look or you go, there will surely be one or two, or maybe more, people that have come from the same country as you.

That should give you a nice feeling, don't you think? There are those who look like you, who talk like you and who crave for the same food as you. What is even more astonishing is to discover that you will hardly have the chance to miss some things or food from back home because they are all in the country you have moved to or can be authentically prepared here.

You will be tempted to want to smile, talk or catch up on stories with these fellow immigrants. However, the reality is, meeting them in a random place only means being able to throw in a half smile and, at most, say hello. While the encounter may be so brief or out of context that there will be no valid reason to hold up the other person, you can ask them for some brief information like directions.

One of the places which could allow more engaging conversations is when you meet them at your kids' school, in a job search workshop, in a class you are attending yourself, in a local or ethnic store. Only then, will you somehow find that they are not strangers after all, but have names and faces, and calling cards, too.

Whether they come from the same country as yours, or share any other commonality, do not hesitate to ask and approach. Only then will you start knowing and learning. For example, because Canada has become so multicultural and full of non-stop migration, everyone is used to being asked for directions on the street, the bus, or the train. The asking could even extend to tips on how to do things, how to find a job, how to segregate waste, how to read your electric bill, how to find the best cable or phone provider or a myriad of other information.

If you do not know something, it is because either you have not asked or have not read at all. I am amazed at how flyers fly everywhere in most points of contact among people. There is your bus schedule, church activities, school calendar, ongoing sale events, employment listings, store directories, course syllabi—just about everything and anything. And we are only talking of paper documents. The information can be even more overwhelming on individual websites.

So whether you choose to deliberately seek out help from people, country-mates or not, you will realize that it will not be difficult to know or catch the needed information. You need only to go out and seek, and ye shall find.

It's sad to say, but it can also happen that some country-mates disappoint you. It is probably not so bad if you are ignored and refused the correct information. But you can also be misled. Yes, there is a snake in every forest, and there will always be bad people.

Sometimes, getting misled or getting the wrong or inaccurate information may not arise out of malice or a bad intention. It's possible that the people you are talking to are no longer in tune with the times. They know only so much and not any better. If it is any consolation, good people still outnumber the bad ones.

I would say it is my own countrymen who helped me settle in my new country and it was a *kababayan* who made that final decision to take me in for my first serious job. In another form, *blood could truly be thicker than water*.

1. *It is always a high probability that you will find country-mates who can help you.*
2. *The key is not hesitating to ask and to know what to ask.*
3. *Good people still outnumber the bad ones, and that is true anywhere in the world.*

5.5   Will Other Cultures Support You?

> THE ENGLISH LANGUAGE, FOOD AND MUSIC ARE THE GREAT MEDIATORS IN EASILY ADAPTING TO OTHER CULTURES. WITH THAT, YOU WILL COME TO REALIZE THAT THE WORLD IS YOUR WHOLE SUPPORT SYSTEM.

Upon arriving here, chances are, for some of your needs, it is not a fellow countryman who has the best answer or who can help you.

Most countries who accept many immigrants have become such a mixture of cultures that even the most basic of your needs can be dependent on the ability or willingness of some other nationals to help you.

I rented my first apartment from a meticulously clean Chinese couple. A patient Korean oriented one of my sons on school admission. My daughter's first best friend in school is half-Dutch. I buy my wet market stuffs from a store run by an enterprising Indian. My first resume coach was an American from Hawaii who I mistook for a Filipina. It turned out that she was Japanese-American raised in Hawaii who then moved to Canada. My officemates and trainers in my first serious job are peoples of varied cultures, and each one went out of his way to help me adjust to my new job.

Although the school environment normally teaches us to respect other cultures and help build a harmonious universe, living abroad actually allows you to come face to face with those lessons. With that, there are so many things to learn, some habits to undo, and new ways to accept.

Living in a multicultural country throws you into this situation. You cannot discriminate and cannot be discriminated upon. The highest respect is given even to the most minority of the visible origins. Speaking in your native tongue in public (meaning if there are other cultures present) can seem impolite as it might be misconstrued as using your language in order to say something derogatory or insulting.

But it is also true that because of a minority status, some people may be so defensive about their cultures that they have the tendency to protect themselves. This could go either way. Some may tend to be arrogant, others too withdrawn. Others will feel superior, others inferior.

In time, you will come to better understand other cultures and they will come to understand yours. All along, each one only desires to be of help to one another, to support one another in an environment that is so new and intimidating. Sometimes the facility of adapting to a new spoken language can be a hindering factor to start understanding.

I feel we need to thank the British about the universality of the English language. At the outset, the English language is the balancing factor. Perhaps, it is the only visible, or rather audible, common factor through

49

which the process of uniting can start. Communications is that important. The second redeeming factor is food. *The best way to a man's heart is through his stomach.* The taste bud can be discriminating, but it is trainable. The taste bud also allows you to be familiar faster without the difficulty of adjustment. I am sure even in our respective native countries, we always try other cuisines. That becomes our shortcut to learning and embracing other cultures.

And of course, there's music. Music transcends boundaries. Music is actually the original universal language. More than the meeting of the minds, it touches on the meeting of the hearts. What could be more powerful than that? We know that the act of helping begins when the need speaks to one's heart.

In reality, if you allow it, the world is your support system. Everyone in it is capable of easing your process of adjustment and adaptability. Again, you only need to ask and you shall find.

1. *In largely multicultural communities, like in Canada, adapting to the many different customs present is a process.*
2. *Other cultures may be different, but they all share the same intention to help.*
3. *The key to getting help is to ask. Asking will be your first lesson in humility.*

CHAPTER 6   YOU NEED LOGISTICS

6.1   What Kind of Accommodations Do You Need?

> IF YOU MOVED TO BUILD A NEW LIFE, THEN START OFF
> RIGHT BY TRYING TO FIND A PLACE YOU CAN CALL HOME.

Many sob stories have been exchanged here and there about families who once lived so comfortably in their native country finding themselves living in humble, freezing basements or square holes called "room-for-rent spaces" in their newfound country.

But migrating puts reality right in front of you. Rather than pity yourself, look at it as being given the chance to live your life all over again, to make new choices, to face up to new challenges, to win new battles and gather new victories.

Looking for the place you can temporarily call your home is indeed a challenge. It requires patience and realistic assessments. Thanks to the internet, even from your home country you can start searching for possible apartments or rooms to rent. A friend from the country you are moving to can then physically check out the locations for you.

All you need is to learn is how to Google: Just type in "apartments for rent in (such and such location or city.)" You will actually find too many websites because renting out is really a big side source of income for established folks. They call it a "mortgage helper." Some are able to pay their monthly mortgage amortization by simply renting out some parts of their houses —rooms, basements, ground floor or upper floor.

Your friend or relative can check out the place and give you feedback.

This process will be even better if you can ask them to take pictures and "show you around" the house. The nice thing about being able to search through the internet is that the rental cost is almost always advertised, so you can filter your choices to only those you can afford.

The close-to-bus stop or close-to-amenities factor is not really as ticklish an issue because Canada, for example, has an efficient public transportation system. The areas are also well zoned so that there will be a school nearby, as well as a church, a mini mall, a walk-in clinic, a public library, just about the most basic services that you will need.

There is not much criteria that you can put up if you are doing it from far away, but you can always move to another place once you start getting acquainted with life in the new place. Ideally, try to find a place that will agree to a short-term lease, such as 6 months, to give you more leeway to move out sooner.

If getting a really comfortable home is not so easy because money is an issue, then it's crucial that the home is filled with enough love, understanding and support for one another. Even if you have to live in a basement, the warmth of home can be felt with the unity and love of family. On the light side of things, even if the weather becomes too cold for comfort, we mentioned somewhere in this book that the key is simply to be able to bundle up properly.

1. *Finding a comfortable home is your first step to starting a new life.*
2. *Migrating brings you face to face with reality and home is the best place to plan for it, strategize for it, savor it or simply chill out after a frustrating day of job hunting.*
3. *You will also find that home is the best place to bring home the bacon when luck comes knocking and you feel you have made the right decision migrating.*

6.2   Hello, Have You Got a Job for Me?

YOU NEED A PHONE. THAT IS AS BASIC AS GETTING A JOB TO FEED YOUR STOMACH.

When we migrated, there was only one important first-step decision that was almost instinctive to me, that was to seek how I could get a phone line. Your cell phone might work through international roaming, but pretty soon you will realize that roaming is expensive and will not get you anywhere near your goals as a permanent resident.

As you settle, or perhaps even before you came over, the need to communicate or stay in touch with people you left behind will be there. That will be first stabilizing factor that will console you as you settle.

However, when things are turning out not in the way that you had imagined or wanted—especially with that first job becoming so elusive—you might find yourself slowly withdrawing from your past, unwilling to speak of the frustration you feel even to friends.

Then you will realize that the connections we are talking about here will focus on the need to spread yourself and gain more knowledge of what is going on around you in this new place that you have moved to. You must use your phone to call friends here to ask for job leads, to call companies regarding possible openings, and to receive invitations to parties where you can meet other people.

Do you need a landline or a mobile phone? A landline will always be cheaper than a mobile phone because it allows you unlimited access to local calls. If you have somebody in the family who can be efficient at taking calls while you are out job hunting or attending workshops, then a landline will be good enough while you are in a tight budget.

My first mistake was getting a mobile post-paid plan only to realize how expensive it ended up being and how little I needed it in the first months that we were here. Nothing beats quick-witted decision-making. Having realized that mistake, I had to compute how much more it would cost me to continue on with the plan against paying the penalty of terminating the contract. I opted out of the contract as soon as I could. I can always get a prepaid cell phone if the need calls for it.

However, if you are single or coming alone, and there is nobody to take calls for you at home, then you have two options: Either make sure your landline phone has a voicemail facility or an answering machine, or secure a mobile phone you can take with you anywhere you go. Since you will be waiting for some calls that may come from jobs you have applied for, make sure your recorded messages are as formal and polite as possible.

If you must buy a mobile phone, weigh very well which plan—whether post-paid or prepaid —will be most economical and efficient for you. Of course, the best is if you are living with a friend or relative or tenant who will allow you to use his landline phone to make some local calls from home. But you cannot expect that generosity every single day.

What could be irritating about some mobile phone systems is that incoming calls will be charged to your credits or to your plan. Certainly, you will not mind if the incoming call is what you expect or wanted, but think of the hundreds of telemarketers who can get hold of your number—no thanks to your phone company who sells your number for a song. That does happen. Find out if there is a Do Not Call List national registry in your new country. Canada has it and you can register your number to minimize uninvited marketing calls.

When making calls for work or job postings, make sure you know what area codes are considered local to the phone you are using. Also seek out for these companies' 1-800 numbers so that your calls will not be considered long-distance calls. Some efficient phone companies will warn you that you have dialled an out-of-area or international number, so that cautions you as to whether you should proceed with the call or not.

1. *The need for communication can never be understated.*
2. *While you need to scrimp, consider getting a phone as basic in your job search.*
3. *Staying connected and reachable will improve your job of job hunting.*

6.3   **What, No Internet Connection?**

THE WORLD HAS NARROWED WITH INTERNET. USE THIS TO YOUR BEST ADVANTAGE, BUT DO NOT THINK THAT THIS IS THE BEST WAY TO FIND A JOB.

Technology has certainly conquered this part of the world. In Canada, statistics show that more than 80% of the population have access to the internet. More than 50% of those people use high-speed internet, and almost 50% are said to connect to internet at least three times a day.

I would say that an internet connection should form part of the basic logistics that you should have upon coming. Needless to say, this includes a laptop or a desktop PC, which you might have brought from home. Even if you haven't, getting yourself a laptop or computer is a necessary investment that you owe yourself.

Whether you are alone or with your family, the best deals are the bundle deals of phone, internet and cable connections. Such bundled products are things you want to have anyway, and better sooner than later, because you need to speed up your search to get that job soon.

The choice between internet service providers is not an area that I will delve into. There are a lot of providers, all with promises of having the best connections. Price will always be a factor I know, but make sure that the low price is not directly proportional to a low quality of connection. In any case, to stay competitive, most companies will not slap any penalty if you decide to terminate your contract and will allow you to opt out seamlessly by just one phone call.

However, do not be distracted by your fascination with internet surfing or social media networking. Always remember that you intend to increase your chances of finding a job through the internet. That should be top-of-mind.

I remember being advised to consider the job search itself as your first job. Set up a corner in your home as your office and keep the things you will need there, or just within arm's reach. The phone should be there, the computer, the notepads, the pencil, the printer, the USBs, practically everything you will need to be comfortable and efficient.

I have warned that any job seeker should not consider internet recruitment as the way to go for all employers, or the best employers. But as you are just starting out, with no connections or network to speak of, a whole gamut of information and potential jobs are there for you for the taking.

It is not necessarily true that there are actually no real jobs to be found on the internet. I should know. Two happy friends got their biggest breaks only by applying through the internet.

1. *You will definitely need to get a high-speed internet connection.*
2. *The internet makes it easy for you to try to find as many job opportunities as you can.*
3. *The use of internet may be convenient, but use it only as a take-off point to find the real jobs that are available and that you want.*

6.4   Have You Visited Your Public Library Lately?

THE PUBLIC LIBRARY IS A TOOL PROVIDED TO YOU. DISCOVER HOW YOU CAN USE IT TO YOUR ADVANTAGE, ESPECIALLY IN YOUR SEARCH FOR THAT FIRST JOB.

Where I came from, I had the feeling that the internet had invaded the functionality of the local library. I never saw, or perhaps never noted, any of my own children having to rush to the school library or stay late studying in a library.

Any trip to the library usually meant first having to check out whether the computer is available for public use. And thus, any research or data gathering needed will be done through the library's computer with its internet connection, and not through the wonderful world of books we know.

Coming to Canada definitely allowed me to rediscover the fascinating world of books at the physical library, in the tradition that we had once known. The thousands of books, tapes and DVDs, publications, magazines, newspapers that abound public libraries are simply awesome. And of course, the internet connection that you need is there, too, if you cannot afford yet to subscribe to one in your own at home.

Having spent all of my waking hours working and thinking about work in my life in my home country, the public library has enabled me to catch up with the world. I read the books that I had always wanted to read, and new ones, too. I watch the best movies I failed to see in my working life. That includes local movies and TV series from my home country. Yes, they have that in their collection, too.

The public library as an organization is not only set up to lend books or DVDs, but is also an entire source of learning to orient you, guide you, improve you and assist you in your migration. Just like how the whole Canadian government, for example, seems to be organized, with many concerns central and focused to the continuous coming and going of people.

It has its own initiatives on job search and similar programs for the smooth integration of new immigrants. It has activities for your children, even contests with welcome prizes. It has its own volunteer mechanism that welcomes both new and existing migrants, enabling them to channel their energy and probably extra time while they are still looking for full-time work.

Getting your library card as soon as you land is probably one of the wisest things that you can do. It is well worth it, whether simply to find a reason to go someplace, interact with other people, or connect to activities in the community that are initiated by the public library as an efficient and effective organization.

As always, that physical library on the block serves as a mute witness to the struggles of people wanting to start a meaningful life abroad. Every day, this witness welcomes everyone with open arms in the comforts of its warm and cozy space just so life can start somewhere and move forward. In the same manner, it serves as a comfortable refuge to those who are taking things slow and easy after a hardworking day or a challenging past life.

1. *Rediscover the use of the library to help you start a life.*
2. *Most public libraries in developed countries have been organized as a dynamic institution that can also address the seamless integration of new immigrants into the community,*

including helping them in their job search.

3. *Get back to the wonderful world of books and see the movies you have missed. This can help ease out the heavy feeling of seemingly endless job hunting.*

6.5   Do You Need a Car?

> A VERY EFFICIENT TRANSPORTATION SYSTEM MAY MEAN THAT YOU DO NOT EVEN NEED A CAR. BUT GETTING A DRIVER'S LICENSE AND OWNING A CAR CAN ALSO GIVE YOU AN EDGE.

The question is pretty straightforward, but let me say that for many who can afford a car, the decision to buy one must still be well-thought-out. Buying one was one of the more costly mistakes that I made after immigrating.

Mistake No.1: I went looking for a nice car to buy even before I could get my driver's license. Obviously, I underestimated the difficulty of passing those road tests and went on to take almost a full year to pass one. That left the car I had purchased to spend one year in the garage accumulating dust or ice, depending on the season.

Mistake No. 2: I got the car even before I found a job, only to realize how burdensome the cost of insurance and maintenance would be. Since I did not want to take that out from my own money, I ended up not insuring the car, although it took me six months to decide that, still hoping that I will pass my road test soon. And so the car continued to rest in the garage for another six months.

Can you afford a car? Of course, I knew I could afford to buy a car, but I opted to borrow instead because interest rates were very low at that time. So, Mistake No. 3: Borrowing and paying for interest for something that I could not use or decided not to use.

So why did I make the mistake of buying a car so soon? Probably, I had it in my heart to continue giving my kids the comfort that they had back home. If there was any personal consolation, I felt it was the only luxury I can afford to assuage my bruised ego of having to come over and have nothing, only to realize that none of these is necessary, at least for the time being. As one sensible friend said, one step at a time.

One thing you will learn trying to start a new life in an organized country like Canada is that there are no shortcuts to anything. If there are, they are more exceptions and may be sheer strokes of luck. Thus, every major decision must be one careful step at a time.

But what does all this have to do with your job hunt? It is to let you know that you do not need the car if you are applying for non-transportation related or non-mobility related jobs. But not getting the driver's license? That seems so basic, and you will realize that some jobs require it. No matter how hard it takes to get one, just keep on trying. I had to take the test five times.

If the transportation system is efficient, you can actually consider never needing your own car. But every time I say that to my kids, they remind me to dream that one day we will need one again because one day we will have the luxury of going out for pleasure or to travel out of town for a much needed R&R. How true is it that all work and no play makes John a dull boy.

But my final verdict is that- if you really do want to learn your way around your new place or discover a lot about it, do not immediately get a car even if you can afford it. My one year of commuting has made me grow a lot, exercise-wise and knowledge-wise.

1. *Remind yourself that you are in a new country, and the old comforts back home may have to wait a while.*
2. *Assess your need for efficient mobility while job hunting and whether it is necessary to get your own car.*
3. *Some jobs may actually require a driver's license and owning a car. Getting that driver's license is a rational decision. Getting that car must be a careful, well-timed decision.*

CHAPTER 7 WHERE HAVE YOU BEEN?

7.1 Have You Been a Tourist Before?

> DO NOT COMMIT THE MISTAKE OF BEING A STRANGER IN YOUR NEW COUNTRY. VISIT AS MANY NICE PLACES AS YOU CAN BEFORE THAT JOB HUNTING KEEPS YOU BUSY.

On the other end of the extreme, some may have psyched themselves up so much that they have already convinced themselves that no time can be wasted in beginning to look for a job. Off they go in a 24-hour stint of planning their moves and assessing their chances of getting that job.

Let me not make judgment of how immediate the need for that job is because I am pretty sure if any of us could truly afford to sit around for a while and savour the moment of new freedom and new environment, we would. Why not? We could have come from a place where hard work was our easy daily companion, by necessity. And for sure, because you had worked hard, you gained this reward of being able to qualify to come as an immigrant.

If you honestly qualified to this immigrant program, chances are you were able to show enough proof that you could sustain yourself and your family for at least 6 months without a job. This is not to say, that you should stretch your luck, but simply to remind you that it would be nice if you got to know the country that you have chosen to embrace for the rest of your life.

Upon arrival, whether you like it or not, you are a tourist in this new place. Tourist comes from the word "tour," implying that you owe it to yourself to make a tour and get acquainted with the place. Not necessarily for the place's sake, although that could come with the immigration program business plan, but more importantly for your own sake.

May I refer again to where I am based—British Columbia, Canada. If you can afford it, visit at least those places that your friends talk about as must-see places, or places that are classified as "you've-never-been-to-Canada-if-you-have-never-seen-them." Some of them may require you travel a few hours or cross the waters, but I guarantee you that these places will make you fall in love with British Columbia. Talk of Whistler and Victoria alone. Some others, you get by simply riding a few minutes in a public bus or the skytrain.

Other would-be immigrants come as tourists before applying or getting accepted as permanent residents. Many of those who do that end up saying that yes, this is the country where I want my whole family to grow and make a life. Not only do they see how beautiful it is, but also how habitable the country is. For example, Vancouver, always voted as one of the top 5 liveable places in the world, has the best climate, especially for those who come from tropical countries. From where I live, nature is at my doorstep.

The other significance of doing this as soon as you arrive is the reality that you may never be able to do it once you start looking for a job. The job hunt can be as consuming as it is frustrating at the beginning. The feeling of frustration can weigh you down so that you do not feel like you will enjoy anything else you see. The passing days without a source of income can also weigh heavily on savings, making touring and enjoying the place the farthest thing from your mind at that point.

When I was doing my tourist thing even only by walking or commuting, the only thing that was always running through my mind was the fact that I was getting more and more convinced that I wanted to live here for the rest of my life. And that life would be complete if I found a job. With my own job, even if it was only a humble job in the beginning, I would be able to sail off and conquer better grounds in this new country that I would eventually call my own.

1. *Touring and seeing your new country should be able to reinforce your decision to come.*
2. *The same can also mean being able to learn and acquaint yourself with your new environment and feel more confident about yourself.*
3. *Be a tourist as soon as you arrive. You may not have the time to do this once the job hunt or the new job starts to consume you.*

7.2   How Hard Have You Explored?

> ONLY WHEN YOU GO AND TRY OUT WHAT YOU THOUGHT YOU COULD NOT DO WILL YOU BE ABLE TO TRULY SAY YOU HAVE EXPLORED AND CONQUERED.

For purposes of discussion, I will differentiate "exploring" from the just-concluded section of "touring" the place. If you had the chance to visit other countries as a tourist, it is easy to understand how one gets into the feeling of being able to love the country by appreciating the different places that you see.

Let me therefore limit our definition of "touring" as referring to your senses of sight and feeling. And the definition of "exploring" references your cognitive and creative senses, both of which have to do with the mind. They can easily overlap because, as always, what you see travel to your mind as well as to your heart. But let us not debate on it for now.

Exploring also implies an inner motive or hidden agenda, in the positive sense of the word, of course. You explore because you have something in mind that you want to accomplish or achieve and not simply to know or to see.

But I wish for you to learn the word "explore" to come to terms with wide-ranging possibilities of being able to put yourself in a match to a job you are looking for, or a job that is waiting out there for you.

When you go out and explore a mall, and wish to get a job, you look around for "Now Hiring" signs and enter the first shop that has one. Without a hiring sign, you can further explore and go in to ask at the cashier's counter that you are exploring the possibility that they are hiring. That was what exactly happened to me in my very first job.

I had landed as an immigrant much, much earlier than one of my college chums, but she got a job as early as one week after she came in and had moved on to a second job after six weeks to get to something nearer what she wanted. At that point, all I had was a list of volunteer works. This is not to say I did not want my volunteer works, I enjoyed and learned from all of them, but my college friend had said it was time for me to be more pro-active in exploring my chances of getting a job.

I promised her that the very next day after our reunion dinner, I would visit one of the biggest malls near my place and enter every store that I fancied. This meant I also wanted to work for a company whose products I wanted or patronized. I anticipated that, as an employee, I would be entitled to a big discount on my own purchases. True enough, I had just entered a third store and as soon as I handed over my resume and described myself, I was HIRED!

Was it luck? Maybe. But that luck would not have come if I did not explore.

Exploring also means shedding off your inhibitions. It is going for something and winning it. Although I was a marketing person for many years, I was never sure if I could sell myself at any instant. Or perhaps I was not sure whether selling myself boldly was something I wanted to do, as if a job meant the world to me. But I did it!

You will never know what in the world is waiting there for you if you will not go out and explore.

1. *To explore is to find out what is out there for you and whether what you wanted is existing there for you.*

2. *Exploring can also mean being able to do what you thought you could not do and actually realizing that it can happen.*
3. *Be proactive. That is the first rule of exploring. Walk the mile and bring home the bacon.*

7.3   Can You Google-Map?

> OUT HERE, YOU ARE REALLY ALONE. ON YOUR WAY TO DROP A RESUME OR MEET UP FOR A JOB INTERVIEW? HELP YOURSELF FIND DIRECTIONS. JUST GOOGLE-MAP IT.

One of the most memorable vacations I had in my life was being able to go with the whole family to Hong Kong one Christmas season. Not only because the place is just so near my country of origin, but also because it is so easy to move around the area with the transportation system being just as efficient as Canada's. Plus the fact that it, to me, was a shopper's haven. And we were all excited to see the nearest Disneyland to my country, notwithstanding we have seen the ones in Florida and Anaheim.

I remember one of my kids saying that he'd probably get lost in his own country but not in Hong Kong, because there are almost fool-proof instructions on how to move around the city, especially in train stations. On the streets, there are tourist guides deployed everywhere to direct you to where you want to go. We were standing on a corner waiting for a bus when one of them approached us and asked where we wanted to go. It turned out we were at a wrong bus stop, and she brought us to the right one around the corner.

Canada, for example, obviously does not have the tourist guides deployed on the streets, but you can always walk up to anyone to ask for directions. Almost anybody, or perhaps everybody, is aware of the fact that this is the land of immigrants and that, on a daily basis, new people find themselves having to get acquainted with the place. Thus, on a daily basis, too, anybody can just walk up to you to ask for help.

With a few exceptions, I find the bus drivers generally receptive to that reality. You can always ask them and they will know. But of course, it is important that you also know where you are going because you will never know when you might meet those few exceptions.

If you can Google-map it, you can find it. This is not an advertisement and I am not being paid by Google to say this—but I attest to the fact that Google Map is perhaps one the best things that ever happened to a stranger like me. Not only am I so poor at directions, but I am also so un-adventurous.

As I have probably mentioned somewhere in this book, migration has a way of changing you as a person. Best of all, it has a way of educating you on many things that you never thought you could know or do.

As I found myself unable to always ask friends to bring me to a place or tell me where a certain place is, I have come to love Google Maps. Life had been easy. Canada's Translink company also has its own mapping or directional interactive systems that can tell you exactly what transportation to take, where, and at what time.

The point that I am driving at is the fact that you do not have to be adventurous or good at directions to be able to find the location of that company which you wanted to apply for or which you saw had a job posted.

Out in a strange country, even with family and friends, consider yourself alone. You need to be able to help yourself, especially to simple things such as knowing where you should go or get to.

1. *You do not need to be adventurous or good at directions to know where you are going. Just go.*
2. *Appreciate the efficient system of transportation to help you do that, plus the fact that there is almost nothing you cannot find through Google Maps.*
3. *Do not be afraid to be alone in a place where almost everybody*

expects to be helping other people daily to find places and directions.

7.4   What Are Friends for?

> GETTING YOUR FIRST JOB MAY BE THROUGH THE
> KINDNESS OF A FRIEND, BUT PUTTING UP WITH AND
> WINNING THIS NEW LIFE IS ALL UP TO YOU.

Certainly, I would say being welcomed by my good friend of twenty years or so upon my arrival was one the best things that ever happened to my family as we were moving in. I shall forever keep that in my heart. It was good because I believe no matter how old you are, how strong, or how boldly you are wont to take challenges, the fear of the unknown will always be there. If you are the head of the family or head of the migrating team, you probably think that this fear is only known to you or felt by you. As the leader, that streak of martyrdom in your veins tells you that nobody should be discouraged or give up because of you.

I would say I can offer two schools of thought to that:

One, it is true that, as a leader, courage and determination should be virtues that you should carry around with you, or rub on to everybody as hard as you can. I do not think I could imagine a leader who'd be first to run away from a challenge or a problem. A leader may not literally be at the head of the pack, but he should very well figuratively be the head of strength and faithfulness to the cause.

Two, human as we are, a leader should not also be afraid to show his own fears and doubts. However, a true leader seeks to conquer those with the help of the whole team. A true leader should not be afraid to show his own weakness, but he should also show that he can overcome, and overcome even better if everybody pitches in.

No matter how many friends we have, from back home or from your new country, you will soon realize that survival will still be your own ballgame. Friends will be there at the beginning, in the middle, and at the finish line. But the whole race is going to be run by you and the team you bring with you.

Where you want to go, what you intend to do, or what you hope to accomplish will be your battle, and you will realize that even the closest of friends will only be at the sidelines. Some will be there to cheer you on, some to pick you up when you fall, and others to redirect you to another path. Whatever role they play, they will not measure up to the major role that you and your team need to play yourselves.

Finding your first job may be through the kindness of a friend, but how long you will stay in that position or how you can move on to the next one will be all up to you.

1. *No matter how good or how strong we are, each one will always have the fear of the unknown.*
2. *Lucky are those who have true friends to hold them by the hand as they try and conquer their fears.*
3. *Regardless of how many friends you have, in the end you will realize that the battle shall only be fought by you and the team that you bring with you, your family.*

7.5   Can You See Clearly Where You Are Headed?

> TIME IS OF THE ESSENCE. THE SOONER YOU ARE ABLE TO FOCUS ON WHAT YOU WANT TO ACHIEVE IN YOUR WORK LIFE, THE BETTER.

Where have you been? How far have you gone? Not necessarily in your job search, but also in your own discovery of the place you have migrated into.

When I was preparing to leave, I thought I knew exactly what I wanted to do. Because I had applied under the skilled professionals category, I was definite about the skills and the competencies that I was bringing with me. I thought that, since I had been approved, this country I was moving to was also convinced that those skills were employable.

This is not to say that there was a mismatch or a mistake at all. It is just that coming here, you could be likened to a child who is brought to a candy store and does not know what candies to buy. There will be candies that are new to you, candies that are all appetizing and offered to you at the same time.

While I had own my dreams or wish list, I came to realize that my wish list was too short after all. There is so much that can be done, studied, trained for, or explored. And the very government makes them all available and reachable to you. All you need to do is decide and decide immediately.

For someone who came somewhere in the last fighting chapter of her work life, it was so heartening to realize that here, age is never an impediment to break new grounds and achieve, plus the fact that most companies do not impose any age to retire. Amazingly, you feel so young and as if Pandora's box has just opened up before you.

Suddenly, the world is your stage.

Hold it. That in itself could present a problem. If you are not able to clearly define who you want to be when you set foot, the myriad of options will only confuse you and make things even more difficult to grasp.

The possibilities that are before you are just that, possibilities. You have to fit in yourself or make yourself fit in. And that should start with defining what you want and knowing exactly where you want to be headed to. For those who are young when they came over, it looks like there is plenty of time. But for those who are not, then time is of the essence.

It is not that you should hurry. The point is for you to be able to focus on what you really want and immediately set sail. Remember, that as the clock ticks, the pension or RRSP ticks. The later you get into a job, the shorter your chances of being able to achieve the retirement that you envision.

1. *Coming to a more progressive country, you will soon discover that it can be a land of great opportunities.*
2. *The myriad of new things you can do or become can confuse you, so define and focus on what you really want and where you want to go.*
3. *Time is of the essence. The faster you can do that, the better the impact on your future and your retirement years.*

CHAPTER 8   IS THE VIRTUAL WORLD YOUR OYSTER?

8.1   Do You Like Surfing?

> THE VIRTUAL WORLD IS THE WAY TO GO, AND YOU WILL GET THERE FASTER AND MORE EFFICIENTLY BY LEARNING HOW TO SURF THE INTERNET.

As a mom, I used to resent the fact that my kids were spending too much time on the internet. Many times I judged that to be aimless, and therefore, a waste of time. Besides, I was being protective that they did not chance upon censorable sites and unduly get exposed to virtual indecencies.

Things seemed to worsen when they started learning all those computer games online. And I had to consistently watch that they did not abuse their time and their health. I sort of panicked when I heard the news of a boy who stayed online straight for more than 48 hours and died. That was a real scare.

We have to live with the fact that, in watching over our children, we can only do so much. It seems almost impossible to ogre on them like a hawk for even a full 24 hours. You just need to trust that you had brought them up well and that you had continuously fed them with sound advice and words of wisdom. Eventually, you will realize that they will learn on their own, like when to stop staying up in front of that computer.

I should say it was my children who patiently introduced me to computers. When I was learning to surf the internet, I started understanding my own children. Time just passed me by without realizing that I had spent three to five hours at the minimum doing that. And the kids started to get right back at me, "See Mom, no eating and no looking at the clock." Gee, how true, and I was loving it.

While we view the world wide web, or the internet for that matter, as a different world in itself, it is there to support us. Anything that is out there can build or destroy us. But when used responsibly, surfing the internet is a tool that makes this information instantly available to us without ever leaving our seats. By that, I was beginning to wonder why, in some offices, employees are not given access to the internet as if their employees believe they will be like small kids who would spend their time gallivanting along the virtual highways.

Also, I thought that I became a better mom or friend because I did not have to bother anybody with my trivial questions, or even the valid ones, because the internet almost always provides the answer to anything.

Coming over to a developed country like Canada almost makes it inevitable for anybody to learn to use the computers and surf. Why, there are even classes that are held in community centers which any adult learner can attend for free. Teaching the use of the computer is also a popular task among new immigrants who want to volunteer for work to gain work experience. It is so heart-warming to see our parents and grandparents attending computer classes, and actually wanting to buy their own PCs, afraid that they cannot compete in time and availability among the younger ones for the use of the computer at home.

To paraphrase a more cruel term, whether you like it or not, you will need to learn to use the computer and surf the internet if you want to compete for those jobs that are available out there. They say, only 20% of available jobs out there are advertised, and perhaps 90% of them can be viewed in job sites and company websites. Like me, you can enjoy your computer and make the most use of it too in your job search.

1. *The computer was invented to be a useful tool, and so was the Internet.*

2. *Learning to surf the internet can open up a whole wide and new world to you and help you with anything, including finding a job.*
3. *Only 20% of available jobs are advertised, and perhaps 90% of them are those you find when you surf the internet.*

8.2   What Is in Your Inbox?

THE EMAILS YOU HAVE LEARNED TO WRITE AND THOSE THAT YOU RECEIVE CAN MEAN SO MUCH IN YOUR OWN ABILITY TO HOLD ON, TO KEEP BELIEVING THAT ONE DAY THAT INBOX WILL CONTAIN AN EMAIL THAT SAYS, "YOU'RE HIRED."

Every time I write a cover letter for a job that I think I really want, my last sentence always indicates that I can best be contacted through my email address. Because I am out of the house almost every day, out looking for a job or volunteering or running some errands, my email address is the most efficient address by which I can be reached.

As soon as I started to love my computer, I was never the same conservative, traditional mom. One of my sons commented that it made him very happy to realize that his mom was into computers because then he felt like his mom was not growing old. While it is good to keep in step with your kids, you owe it actually to yourself to keep up to date with the world.

I used to have a job that required me to travel a lot, not only within my own country, but overseas as well. For a budget-conscious person, I did more emailing than doing expensive phone calls or texting to be able to check on the office, the house and my friends. And certainly, I am not a person of few words, so email is just perfect.

But that was not how I got started on the email bandwagon. The office set it up and required that the company go paperless. So memos, reports and proposals began being sent via email. Notations, corrections, and approvals were also emailed, and to show your proofs or confirmations, you could just print the email approval and presto, the project was on its way.

Pretty soon, you will come to realize how easy the internet has made life for all of us.

Nowadays, companies advertising through the internet, also use the internet to receive applications via email, or the more sophisticated ones have interactive application process set up in their sites. Answering to a job posting has been made so easy with the email function of the internet, but it has also made it difficult to compete for attention.

A friend who advertised for a job just to test how much competition she would have after sending an email application, found that in less than 40 minutes that she put out the want ad, more than 300 emailed applications rushed to her inbox. Another employer related that in less than 24 hours, he had more than 1500 resumes in his email address, and he kept wondering how he would be able to read all of them.

If you have written your cover letter and resume well, then chances are it is in the same inbox where you will receive an invitation to come over for an interview. All these are separate topics in themselves, but suffice it to say that while learning to send those email applications are good, be very sure that what you send can be worth reading or can catch attention.

Be careful what you press Send. That Send button in the email address is so critical that you should really exercise caution before pressing the Send button. The past mistake of sending a wrong cover letter you had intended for another job can ruin your chances for a job that you really want, even though you had sent the right resume.

What I do to avoid this is make my cover letter the first page of my resume. In this way, I am able to make sure that I have the right combination of cover letter and resume. This should also give you a little edge because they say addressees sometimes never get to reading your resumes after reading the first one or two paragraphs of your cover letter. Some never get as far as opening your attachments at all.

Learning to email is one of the best things that you could do to make your life, not only your job search better. In between those frustrating job postings that you have replied to, an incoming hello email from a friend back home can get you back on track again and renew your spirit. Sending an email is simply just like writing a letter. It can be therapeutic. It can work for you in many ways.

1. *Learning how to email is a necessary function that internet can allow you to do through your computer if you want to make the most out of it.*
2. *Emailing job applications can be very competitive, but it is totally possible to get a job by responding to an Internet posting.*
3. *The emails in your inbox are like your traditional snail letters, only faster. They can serve to strengthen you despite frustrating job search as you keep receiving hello mails from friends and families who care about you.*

8.3   What? Internet Technology Is 50 Years Old?

WE NEED TO BE ABLE TO USE THIS TECHNOLOGY TO OUR BEST ADVANTAGE. SUCCESS STORIES OF JOBS FROM INTERNET POSTINGS EXIST.

That famous free encyclopaedia on the internet, called Wikipedia, still is the most accessible source of quick and concise information about many things, including the word "internet". May I quote -

*"The **Internet** is a global system of interconnected computer networks that use the standard Internet Protocol Suite (TCP/IP) to serve billions of users worldwide. It is a network of networks that consists of millions of private and public, academic, business, and government networks of*

local to global scope that are linked by a broad array of electronic and optical networking technologies.

The Internet carries a vast array of information resources and services, most notably the inter-linked hypertext documents of the World Wide Web (WWW) and the infrastructure to support electronic mail ...

The origins of the Internet reach back to the 1960s when the United States funded research projects of its military agencies to build robust, fault-tolerant and distributed computer networks.

This research and a period of civilian funding of a new U.S. backbone by the National Science Foundation spawned worldwide participation in the development of new networking technologies and led to the commercialization of an international network in the mid 1990s, and resulted in the following popularization of countless applications in virtually every aspect of modern human life ..."

Therefore, the internet is going 50 years. Yet, many of us are just learning to use it. Where have we been all this time? Well, I don't mean those under 50 or 40 years old. I would surmise that if one is in his 20s or 30s, he must have been living all this time in the technology of the future and the virtual world of the internet. How lucky could one get!

This is not to say that our folks from way, way back were not able to function effectively and efficiently during their own time because they did not have the internet. After all, they were the ones that laid the cornerstone that allowed these technological developments, and how amazing they would be. They, working from so limited resources, were able to hand us down this wonder we now call the internet.

With this technology, we have been enabled.

The world literally opened in the comforts of our home – networking, advertising, studying, connecting, shopping, and job-hopping. Some have surmised that the ease of getting into another job or business opportunity has literally made some workers less restless about their jobs because at a click of a mouse, they know they can find another that needs their skills. The opposite may also be true, just the same.

But pretty soon, you learn that it is that same popularity of the internet that will be its own weakness when trying to put you in a job. As we mentioned, competition is so stiff that you hardly have the best luck in the world for your email or registered application to be noticed. Some job advertisers never get to read hundreds and thousands of resumes that literally come in by the seconds.

On the other hand, I know of real success stories that started with replying to an internet job posting. Maybe luck? The truth is, there are probably ways of doing it right. This will be the subject of the ensuing discussions. Suffice it to say, now that internet technology is here, use it to your advantage.

1. *The geniuses before us created this wonder of technology called the Internet out of the limited resources in their hands.*
2. *We owe it to them and to ourselves to use this technology to optimize the opportunities we can gather from it.*
3. *Finding a job through the Internet can be a challenge, but success stories from it are also as true and real.*

8.4   How Do You Use the Internet Efficiently?

> LEARN HOW USE THE INTERNET TO YOUR ADVANTAGE, NOT ALLOWING THE INTERNET TO TAKE ADVANTAGE OF YOUR ADDICTION TO IT OR IGNORANCE ABOUT IT.

Look, Ma, errr, I mean, Look, Son, I am teaching them now how to use the internet and how to do it effectively. Well, that's me. Any chance by which I can learn and master something, I faithfully go for it. So can you.

Like any piece of new equipment, a new book or a new place, the only way by which you can maximize the use of it is to study it, and use it again and again. This is notwithstanding having to commit errors the first or second time.

But so unlike new equipment or a new book, studying how much use this technology is to you may be a never-ending adventure. Somebody has estimated that there are already close to a billion topics that can be searched in the internet. That does not double count those which are discussed in several other ways by different authors, bloggers, or writers.

The key is to be able to use your search engine efficiently. As I have already mentioned earlier, I am not about to advertise Google, but it has so far been the most reliable search engine that I have tried. I know because I sometimes try other engines, and more often than not, the response I get is "The Host does not exist" or "Page cannot be displayed". How do you search for a topic in the internet without getting the clutter? Keywords are very important. But the more specific you can type in the subject matter you are looking for, the better. An average of six to eight key words will likely get you good results. If you have a question in mind, type it as a question like you would do when you ask someone. Example, "How can I find a marketing job in Vancouver?"

If you are looking for a job, be specific about the job and the place where you prefer to work, even if you still do not have a company in mind. Just as there is what you call the hidden job market which you cannot find even through the internet, there is also what you call "hidden" job sites on the internet. These are the less popular ones, but nevertheless post their own need for job seekers. By searching "How can I find a marketing job in Vancouver," I easily found a head-hunter and executive search agency called GoldBeck that I had never encountered before.

Of course, at this time and age, you should also be able to distinguish and sense the bogus offers and the fraudulent sites. Actually, your computer or the internet has already a way of warning you that a site is potentially fraudulent. My Mac Pro tells me that.

While the internet can be fascinating, I do not advise that you embrace it like it was the only useful thing in the world. I still resent the fact that my kids spend too much time in front of their computers. They never want to visit the library, learn on the job, ask an elder, or simply observe the world around them.

Like any other invention, there can be abuses in its use and abuses to you as a result of your over-indulgence. Who among us has never heard of scams in the internet, in emails or text messaging? The point is simply to ascertain that technology works to your advantage and not technology to take advantage of your addiction or ignorance.

When you see, for example, a job posting in a not-so popular site, proceed to search the company website. From there, navigate to Contact Us to find out the address and if it can be reached by telephone. If it can, try making a call to inquire whether they posted something on the internet and whether the job is still available.

You may also venture to ask whether they will accept a drop-in resume or a mailed-in resume, knowing full well your emailed resume can be drowned in the deluge of responses that the posting may receive. I have done that. It gives you a better feeling to proceed with your application to that company because at least then you have matched a voice to the company. When you choose to actually visit the office, you have effectively put a face to it too.

In a very simple way, you will have used the internet efficiently in your search for a job.

1. *Like any new gadget or piece of equipment, it takes practice to learn how to use the Internet to your advantage.*
2. *How to use it effectively can itself be searched on the Internet.*
3. *The internet does not have to immobilize our creative thinking. You need also to use your discretion and resourcefulness in trying to find the legitimate jobs from the thousands that are advertised in it.*

8.5   Do You Need to Invest in Technology?

> ANY JOB SEEKER WHO WANTS TO STAY ON TOP OF HIS GAME MUST ADMIT THAT HE CANNOT IGNORE TECHNOLOGY. BUT SINCE HE ALSO CANNOT BEAT IT, HE IS BETTER JOINING THE DEVELOPMENT THAT IT BRINGS ABOUT.

There is no stopping technology, just as there is no escaping it. That's the pill you need to swallow, though it is not necessarily a bitter one.

Out here in a developed country, it does not matter what your age is. You just need to embrace what developments technology has laid out for you in order to stay on track, keep in step and most especially, stay ahead. But you also need to invest.

There are three types of investments you need to make.

One, you need to invest time.

Time is probably the only resource we have that we need not pack to carry along with us. We have it and we have it as soon as we step down from the plane. It travels with us every day, wherever we decide to go. However, we should also know that time is the only resource that we cannot retrieve after spending it. This is a most important lesson I always tell my children. While time is a resource we carry along, it is not as if we can get it back once we have given it away, or worst, lost it. Shopping to me has never been so practical than in this side of the world where I can return and get full rebate for things I bought that I have changed my mind about or did not need after all. Unfortunately, that does not apply to spending time itself. You can never bring back the hands of time. This is probably the reason why I love the movie, *Somewhere in Time*. And this is also the reason why I cried in that movie, when the lead actor pulled out a present-day coin which he carelessly left in his pocket, pulling him back to the present time and unable to go back to a most-cherished chapter of his past love life.

The only point I am saying is, if you will need to learn a craft, a trade or a discipline, start as soon as you can. Time is important. Time can be your ally, but can also be your foe. Well, it may seem that way, because no matter how you want it, whatever time you have lost you cannot recover. *Time will never wait for yo*u. And even if you had the money, you cannot buy it or extend it.

Two, you need to invest effort.

If you had made it here, there is no doubt that you are the type of person who makes a great effort to get what you want. You are someone who exerted enough effort to complete all the requirements to immigrate, because the documents are really cumbersome and many. Many people have expressed a desire to make it here. Some of them are qualified, but few take the real effort to start the process.

Your time plus the effort you put into something you want to do or learn or both will make a lot of difference. On average, time is directly proportional to effort. More time means more effort exerted. For the fast learners, less effort and less time may be all it takes.

Three, you need to invest money.

As I mentioned earlier, lessons on how to use the computer and some its functionalities may be obtained for free. In Canada, there are continuing studies program for adult learners in most community centers. But the best things in life are not free. You might have to start thinking of putting in your own money to be able to advance further to give yourself a little cutting edge.

You will realize that competition for jobs is really stiff. To be able to give yourself a fighting chance or stay on top of your game, you have to foresee how much your investment can give you back in terms of job advancement or a new job opportunity.

Investing in technology using your own money may also mean you need to make sure you have your own computer to use every day. Again, you can do that for free in public libraries, but there is greater effort in having to leave the house and queue for your turn at the library, which may be limited to one hour. If you are into computers, you will of course realize that one hour is too short.

The world is moving fast. Developed countries move even faster. Remember—your time, effort and money make up the investment that you will need to keep up with the pace.

1. *We just have to live with the fact that technology has made this world move fast.*
2. *Developed countries move even faster and we need to stay on track, keep in step, and, if possible, move ahead of the game.*
3. *Time, effort and money are investments we need to put in to do that.*

CHAPTER 9   NETWORKING DOES IT

9.1   How Many Times Did You Feel You Were Alone?

> MIGRATING, WITH OR WITHOUT YOUR FAMILY, STILL MAKES YOU FEEL ALONE SOMETIMES. BUT SOON YOU WILL DISCOVER THAT THERE ARE PEOPLE AND THERE IS A LIFE OUTSIDE OF YOUR PREVIOUS ONE.

I trust that anybody who has been approved as a principal immigrant, whether out of sponsorship or independent application, is somebody who is determined, persistent, brave and strong-willed. He is also a type of person who knows what he wants and will work for what he wants. Such being, he is willing to go to great lengths, to walk the mile to get there.

I really, really admire the bravery of people who migrate, who do not even have any relatives or friends to welcome them or assist them in beginning their new life. It is hard enough that you are coming to a strange place, and it is worse if you are a complete stranger in this new place.

Call this extreme, but I should say coming over was to me like going through what they call the different emotional stages of cancer— Denial, Anger, Bargaining, Depression and Acceptance. This is more scientifically known as the Kubler-Ross Five Emotional Stages of Grief. The author Kubler-Ross originally applied this theory to people suffering from terminal illness and eventually to just about anybody who is experiencing personal catastrophe (death, loss of job, income or freedom, etc).

As unique human beings, the stages to be cited may not come chronologically or end for you. Some may stay at different lengths of time at every stage, or may even go back and forth at some stages. But the conclusion is we need to be able to go through all the stages to be able to experience full healing. Only with healing can we begin to live life again to its fullest. So, what are these stages?

DENIAL in the Big C is not accepting the fact that you have it. "No, this could not be happening to me." To me, denial in this situation is sometimes, or perhaps just at the early stages, not being able to accept the fact that suddenly all things seem to be behind you now.

You are left with memories and are confronted by a blank wall, not knowing for sure where to start or how to start all over again. Perhaps fear grips you and you want to believe that this could not be happening, and is probably just a dream. If the first few months become really difficult, then you become angry.

ANGER, not necessarily in the sense that you do not like what has happened or where you have ended up to, and not in the cancer sense in which the afflicted questions God why, of all people, you got the big C. But more of anger in the sense that you are questioning yourself as to whether the decision to go and turn your back from your past life was the right decision.

This is anger in the sense that you are wondering whether you are sick with masochism because, perhaps from a life of comfort, you moved to a life of self-sacrifice. Suddenly the word sacrifice hits you in the head. You remember that you said you were willing to sacrifice everything because you are doing this for your children or your family and not for yourself alone. You come face to face with the reality that you cannot do this alone, but with family, and better yet, with your God. So you decide to bargain.

BARGAINING is striking a deal, perhaps promising to be good if you do well. Begging, praying, wishing. Doing something for the sake of getting something in return. "I am willing to take this menial job, with a meagre salary just to be able to pull us through." I will do this for only three years until I get my citizenship, and then go from there." "I just need to see my children graduate from college or get their own job, and I will be fine." "I promise to bear every pain and sacrifice so that my children can have this opportunity for a better life, just help me get a job, please."

Usually the deal is made with the Higher Being to whom the individual's faith lies. In return, you promise to be a better mother, a better friend, or a better worker.

DEPRESSION is an overwhelming stage. I would think that everyone who gets completely uprooted goes through depression, but at different levels of intensity. Such intensity, I believe, depends on a person's strength of character and faith in his God. Such intensity also spells the difference of how long you are going to stay in this stage. Some may even call for professional help. But never look at it as a sign of mental illness. It is a natural response to a great personal catastrophe.

At this stage, you may feel numb, totally out of control. All the bitterness, anger, pain, frustration and helplessness may overcome you. But as we are taught, an ounce of prevention is worth more than a pound of cure. To me, the cure starts with the awareness that it could happen and trying to keep yourself busy. The environment and quality of life in Canada, for example, is such that it is to your own fault if you have nothing to do—with or without pay.

ACCEPTANCE is different from a feeling of resignation. Resignation may come in the form of bearing the situation in silence and moving on as if drifting or simply coasting along. Acceptance here is making a conscious decision: Accepting that you have now entered into a new reality. Acknowledging that your past life is gone, that you and your family's lives may be forever changed. You then need to re-adjust your life, re-organize tasks, re-assign new roles to yourself and to your loved ones.

But the best part of Acceptance is realizing you can make new connections, new relationships, new interdependencies, new friendships. And that in this, you can also be happy. And that you can start this new life and re-enter the workforce either in an entirely new role or function and can hope to like it, be the best in it, and make a living out of it, surrounded by newfound friends and relations.

1. *In the extreme, many consider migration as a personal "catastrophe," not necessarily in the sense of wreck or damage to one's future life but instead sudden loss of a past life.*
2. *As such, it presents a situation in which one has to undergo the five natural states of emotional grief - Denial, Anger, Bargaining, Depression and Acceptance - to eventually experience complete healing.*
3. *And the best result of healing is being able to hold the new reality hand in hand with new relationships and friendships, and able to function in a new role.*

9.2 How Many New Friends Have You Made?

NEW FRIENDS YOU MAKE MAY BE KEY TO FINDING THE RIGHT JOB THAT MATCHES YOUR SKILLS. THE MORE FRIENDS, THE HIGHER YOUR CHANCES OF FINDING IT.

The old saying does not state, "Tell me how many friends you have and I will tell you who you are."

It simply says, *"Tell me who your friends are and I will tell you who you are."*

Thus, a person starting all over again has this one great chance to once more start accumulating friends, but this time with full awareness and maturity to discern the kind of friends he should nurture and keep, the maturity to know that it is never a matter of quantity, but instead is a matter of quality.

Or perhaps, you can go by the rule of the smart lover who says "Collect and collect, and then select." Many friends may come by you. Accept them but eventually filter them as to those which ones you'd keep close to your heart. In fact, sometimes you do not even have to do your own elimination process because eventually the number will dwindle as the not-so-true ones slowly drift away by themselves.

But I hope you never for once thought that friends are going to drop from heaven for you. You may have one or two that you knew from way back home, but that is not going to multiply by itself when the rain comes and they get wet like gremlins. You need to go out and meet them.

Upon arrival in Canada, I was pleasantly surprised to find out how many compatriots I do have in this country. I met them everywhere I went. I knew them by their nose or perhaps color, or maybe I just knew. However, looking back, I realized that the most that I could do then was look them in the eye and give out a half-smile. While they may want to engage you in a conversation, there are probably a lot of things going on in their minds or maybe both of you are rushing somewhere and you can only hope to see them around again sometime.

You are really not able to stop and talk to them until they become your church-mates, officemates, schoolmates or community volunteer-mates. You need to find occasions to meet them and be able to make friends. I would surmise that a lot of those who used to be introverted or withdrawn start to learn to come out of their shells in order to know people, to network and spread themselves.

Many studies on job searches say that networking is still the most effective way to get the job you want. For a lot of survival jobs, you do not need any network to be accepted into. You must simply walk in to any store you want and ask if they are hiring. Chances are you will hit upon one that could end up as your first employer.

But to be able to hit upon the job that is in line with the skills that you have brought with you or near the line of work that you used to do back home or were trained for, you need to be able to chance upon the right people to help you or open doors for you. But these right people can be new friends or friends of new friends.

By simple mathematics, the more new friends you make, the higher your chances are of hitting upon the right job that matches your skills or credentials. The more people you come to know, the more referrals you will gain. There is, however, an investment of time and effort that has to be made. The more time and effort you invest, the more you gain people's trust and confidence because they get to have first-hand knowledge of observing you at "work" or working with you on a project.

1. *You need to go out and spread yourself to be able to increase your network of new friends.*
2. *Invest time and energy in your community where you will meet people who might be key in helping you find the job that you really want.*
3. *Only when you are able to exhibit your capacity or ability to do certain things well will you gain the trust and confidence of people who may speak well of your abilities to others.*

9.3   What About Your Old Friends?

KEEP OLD FRIENDS AS THEY CAN BE THE KEY TO FINDING YOUR FIRST JOB, OR MAYBE YOUR BEST JOB.

I always believe that good friends are your true wealth.

I can't be naive to say that that means you can count on them when you are broke, financially. As a matter of fact, you can't. Or you shouldn't.

I do not know, but I have this horrible feeling when I think of having to borrow money from friends. If they volunteer to lend to you, maybe. But you shouldn't count on them or to run to them when you need financial help. After all, they are your friends, and it is not good to take advantage of friendship in that sense. Also, it is not good to lose that friendship for that reason.

For the many happy thoughts and nice things you and your friends have shared together, causing a rift because of that lowly dollar or any other currency is not worth it. While we all need money to survive, money is the nastiest reason to lose friends. If for any reason you had to borrow from a friend, keep the trust and be really thankful.

Friends may volunteer to help you but you will realize in the end that they may also withdraw that help from you. And that is the point that I do not want to see or ever be part of, because it hurts, no matter how politely or cleverly it is done. And the worst part is, you can never show how you really feel about it because you also do not want to hurt in return. It's a plain and simple fact of life.

But that is about money, cold money.

So, my advice is, before you come to the point where you will need to borrow money, seek friends instead to help you find a way to earn money, to find a job.

Friendships made from back home, whether the people are here or there, can be your first source of information or tips on job prospects. They can always refer you to some connections or knowledge of available jobs or good employers.

With the internet and email, being able to network or increase your network through friendships you have made in your "former" life is easy and quick.

My very first direct contact with a Canadian company was by way of an email introduction to a former colleague of a friend back home. It paved the way for my resume to get to the HR and head of the unit I was applying with, and my eventual completion of all the tests and interviews. That initially gave me an idea of the hiring process in Canada. Believe me, however, when I say that technology can never replace human, face-to-face interaction or introduction. This is still the best thing that works. Being personally introduced to a prospective employer or a contact to the employer is perfect.

Why would employers want to hire someone that way? Because employers prefer people whom they can trust. If they are referred by people they also trust, the less work they have in having to background check or credit investigate an applicant. They save time and money that way.

And why would you also want to be hired that way? Because you also need an employer you can trust. An employer who will not short-change you. Someone who is fair. Someone who will not make your period of adjustment more difficult than it already is.

1. *Keep friendships forever. It is always wise to keep adding, rather than subtracting.*
2. *Your old friends may be able to help you find your first job or probably even your best job.*
3. *Employers prefer hiring referrals because they need people they can trust. In the same tone, your adjustment to your new life will be easier if your first job is with an employer you can also trust.*

9.4 Have You Looked for a Group to Join?

> WHERE YOU ARE IS YOUR DESTINY. WHAT YOU WILL BE IS WHAT YOU DO WHERE YOU ARE.

Where do you usually meet people? While I said that people will not drop from heaven at your feet, I believe you are destined to meet them. However, that destiny will not look for you. You must search for your destiny. Is there a contradiction in the phrase "searching for your destiny"? Doesn't destiny simply find you?

You are where you should be. That, I believe, is your destiny. But finding people and circumstances in this destiny requires that you be able to perform your role in this very destiny. And primarily, your role is to go out and believe that, somewhere out there, you will meet the right people who will be instrumental in fulfilling the purpose of this destiny, in realizing your dreams and plans in this new life.

You need to go out, talk to people, and find things to do with people.

Canada, for example, as a land of immigrants has evolved through the years. Its society and environment have developed to respond to the needs and expectations of the people it attracts. This is happening both in governmental and the private sector, including non-profit and community organizations. As such, you will find it so heart-warming to realize that many of these organizations are so structured as to welcome new settlers and smoothly integrate them into a multicultural society.

It is not bad that the natural tendency of new immigrants is to look for people or organizations made up of their own kind, race, religion or color. If it will be the best and quickest way to integrate, then why not? You will not be surprised to find out that there are indeed many organizations made up of your own people, sometimes as many as there are ethnic groupings within your own home country.

Religion, on the other hand, is probably the biggest communal commonality there is. When we think of other countries where the practice of your own religion might be prohibited or banned, we would be so much grateful at the freedom of religion in a country like Canada. All denominations of religion are aptly represented and allowed to be pursued as a basic human right, even the "practice" of no religion at all. So, one of the very firsts groups that you may find yourself affiliated with could be your own church or place of worship.

Remember, however, that when you migrate, you will inevitably live in a multi-cultural society. As such, it is good to join groups that are multi-cultural. The sooner you decide to integrate yourself this way, the better you will understand other people and the better you will be able to harmonize with them when you find them in the workplace. Many times in our day-to-day lives, we spend more quality and waking hours with people at work. This spells the importance of working at being able to learn how to deal and mingle with other cultures.

Then there are professional organizations specific to your career, like those for accountants, marketing, IT experts, lawyers, nurses, doctors, caregivers to name a few. It is of course smart to join these types of groups, especially if you want to rub elbows and meet new acquaintances of people in the very industry where you intend to build or to grow in your career.

Socio-cultural affiliations are another thing to look into. Coming to Canada made me realize how one's quality of life can be so upgraded by your community. The community centers are amazing. The line up of activities and the facilities that are open to you for free or with a minimal fee cater to building up a very healthy and wholesome life. In these community centers, you will meet all kinds of people, future friends and maybe future employers or co-workers.

Whether it is for social, cultural, religious or professional reasons, soon you will realize, it does not matter. Just join. Inevitably, your mission of finding the right job might be accomplished by joining one of these organizations.

1. *Your host country might be huge compared to where you have come from. But this new place is your destiny.*
2. *What you will be depends on what you do, the people you meet, and the groups you choose to join.*
3. *Whether the choice of group is based on any factor—race, religion or profession —keep your focus on your mission, that is, to find the job that you want, no matter how long it might take or how difficult it might be.*

9.5   **How Do You Approach People for a Job?**

FINDING WORK THROUGH NETWORKING IS NOT AS EASY AS THE PEOPLE YOU MEET HOLDING THE JOBS IN THEIR HANDS AND HANDING IT TO YOU. IT STILL BEGINS WITH WHAT YOU HAVE IN YOUR OWN HANDS.

Prior to my migration, I never had any experience in looking for a job. My very first job came to me immediately after graduation from the university as an honour graduate recruit of the then state bank in my country. The next one after that was a result of being pirated by another bank after having been discovered in a collaborative effort of four big banks to put up a shared switch system for their network of Automated Teller Machines. The last one before I immigrated was through a merger acquisition.

I have to admit, every time I felt bad about my work or my boss, I flattered myself by floating around my resume to competitor banks. But I never really considered leaving or entertaining any offer seriously. That was just my way of convincing myself that I could still sell myself and that some company out there was willing to buy. After that, I would feel good and get back to my job in my usual form.

Resume writing was not something I was an expert at. It just so happened that my resume, modesty aside, was power-packed. I was fortunate enough to have gotten the best education and had been given very challenging assignments that helped build up my career in marketing and communications. Therefore, in whatever way I wrote my resume for as long as I was "pretending" to apply in a bank then, I had the privilege of being invited to an interview. It never failed. I mean, my resume never failed me.

Finding myself in the real job jungle out here after immigrating, I have already lost count of the number of versions of resume I have saved as Word files. My classmates and I, in a resume writing workshop I attended, would email each other and joke about the hundredth version of resume we were in the process of writing or sending out.

I know the rule about being able to customize your resume to the position and job description you are responding to. But because it does seem like a miracle to find a job that exactly fits your skills and qualifications when you come in, you appear to have no choice but to apply for a job that only touches on one or two of the skills that you have, maybe not even the best skills that you think you have.

Whether you are hoping for that miracle or simply hoping to get any job, the number of people you know and have met will certainly open more doors for you and will spell a lot difference in your job search. That is networking in this sense.

If you come alone or with only a handful of friends or relatives, networking is obviously something you will work on over time but it should be worth your time and effort.

The math is simple. The wider your network, the more opportunities you will know about, and possibly the higher the chances you will have of getting a job. Companies prefer to hire referrals, we have said earlier, because they want people they can trust. It also saves them the effort of having to background check and investigate as hard.

But finding work through networking is not as easy as the people you meet having the jobs in their hands and handing it to you. It is not as simple as walking up to the new friend and asking "Do you know of any hiring in your company or elsewhere?" I would personally look at it as abrasive or even distasteful if that happened too soon, after only a few hi's and hello's.

I believe in waiting to pop the magic question until you have been able to prove yourself as a reliable, hardworking and trustworthy person to work or deal with. Meaning, your attributes must show. It will also take being able to exhibit the skills that you have and create a "demand" for these skills. It will take a few meetings and working in projects together. Lastly, your sincerity and genuineness must be felt by those people around you.

Even if you had those, the manner and the occasion with which to pop out the question still calls for a lot of tact and prudence. That should be easy to understand if you put yourself in the place of the person being asked. It is a turn-off to be bothered with that question at any place or time.

On your part, even if you need a job badly, keep your dignity intact, especially if that is all that you have for now. There is another time and job search technique (walking-in) where your aggressiveness can work well for you and you have the luxury of not minding what the other person thinks momentarily, but we will discuss that in another chapter.

1. *Networking is acknowledged to be the best strategy of finding a job.*
2. *Networking is like gathering pebbles on the seashore. You have the choice to choose the ones that attract you and the ones you want to keep.*
3. *Networking will only be effective if you have been able to convince your new friends or acquaintances that you have the right skills and attributes to be recommended for a job. Sometimes, you may not even have to ask.*

CHAPTER 10   VOLUNTEERISM IS IT

10.1   What is Volunteerism?

> VOLUNTEERING IS NOBILITY AT WORK, BUT THE SAME
> NOBILITY HAS BEEN DESIGNED TO PREPARE YOU TO FIT
> AND FIND THE JOB THAT WILL MATCH YOUR SKILLS.

The world witnessed for the first time how volunteerism put a president in the Oval Office. The Obama volunteers, said to have numbered in the millions during his campaign, not even counting his social networking fans, successfully worked together to defy history and barriers of colors and beliefs. By the same token, the Obama campaign defined victory for volunteerism, that volunteerism can be a key ideology and strategy for success.

Volunteerism in the community is engaging a citizen to work without the benefit of material returns to oneself, but to simply give one's time and effort freely to build a strong and self-reliant community. Volunteerism is the heart of community development and services.

In Canada, some people even say that you cannot even call yourself "Canadian" if you have not volunteered for anything at all. Across this country, there was once a study that showed that volunteers had rendered more than 2 billion hours of work that was equivalent to 1 million full-time jobs. There was at one point twelve million individual volunteers in more than 150,000 charitable and non-profit organizations, generating more than $100 billion in one year for Canada.

Thus, it can also be said that the arms of official and non-profit governance have definitely benefitted materially from the acts of volunteerism of citizens, who are reported to render an average of 96 hours of volunteer work a year. As such, these organizations themselves recognize the need of these volunteers to gain from the experience and get credited for the services rendered.

But let me just state that it is important to examine your objectives when volunteering for an organization. Whether I like it or not or whether you like it or not, there are two levels of objectives that may surface—one that goes for the altruistic reasons, and the other for personal reasons. Just as any organization will be so happy to accept you as a volunteer, be happy likewise with the fact that the volunteering will be mutually beneficial.

I do not exactly feel comfortable with talking about volunteerism as a strategy to find a job. To me, volunteerism is a sacred act and the nobility of its purpose is not to be misappropriated as a trick or a technique to a motive. Even if such motive is meant to feed one's family or spell one's survival in an economic society.

But what I believe does not matter, because nature rules that *what comes around, goes around.* What you have given will come back to you in ways you may never have planned or imagined. Thus, whether or not you intend to look at volunteerism as a springboard to a future job opportunity, the fruits of your genuine labour will come back to you a hundredfold.

This organization you are serving as a volunteer may not have that real job for you. But as you hone your skills and gather enough exposure, there will be one waiting for you out there. Believe that. As a person, I know it would feel a lot better if I don't expect those whom I had helped to return my kindness, but something or somebody else will in perfect time.

1. ***Volunteerism is engaging the benevolence of citizenry to build a strong and self-reliant community.***

2. *Volunteering may be to you a way to integrate usefully into this society and meet people of varied cultures.*
3. *Whether you ask for it or not, the fruits of good volunteer works will return to benefit you and your job search objectives.*

10.2   Why and Where Should You Volunteer?

THE FIRST RULE IS TO FIND AN ORGANIZATION THAT INTERESTS YOU, OR WHERE YOUR INTERESTS AND TALENTS CAN BE USEFUL AND HONED.

Giving one's time for free is noble in itself, and hundreds of organizations out there are waiting to be beneficiaries of this worthy gesture. For that reason, any group or organization that you choose must be willing to take you and you will certainly mean a lot of help to them.

However, as an individual, you owe it to yourself to find your interest. You do not volunteer to a sports association if you are not the athletic person. Since you are not being paid, you should at least enjoy being in it. What you see, what surrounds you, and what you expect to accomplish must be worth looking forward to each day that you go out and proceed to this office or venue. And most of all, you should also be able to make use of your talents while doing work for it.

Some volunteers take the effort further by choosing to volunteer in organizations or specific offices where they want to be hired for a job when opportunity presents itself. Is that bad? No, just smart, as long as you never lose your good intentions and faithful service.

Above altruism and all, there are two personal objectives that should generally guide you in volunteering: firstly, to be able to apply your skills and hone them in the process; and secondly, to meet as many people as possible in your new community.

You have always heard about the term "global" and have spoken about it like you know it means thinking about the world within your grasp. But the reality of going global happens when you meet peoples of several nations every single day, as you ride the bus, walk in the mall, dine in the food court, celebrate mass, go to a PTA meeting, hand in a resume, do your grocery, make a call, do your volunteer work.

This being said, any volunteer work will enable you meet all kinds of people, people of differing race, color or religion. However, the more significant part of it is how the volunteer work will make you understand them and start to learn to live more harmoniously with them.

Even I realized that, until you find yourself in this situation, you will never know how to act and react. When you are in your own country, where you consider yourself dominant or even a first-class citizen, you do not find the need to ever learn about other races or adjust to them. At the back of your mind, the adjusting is not yours to initiate or even do at all.

Canada, being called the great land of immigrants, pushes you right in the middle of this dilemma. It almost leaves you no choice but to make the adjustments to people of different cultures because you will co-exist with them for the rest of your life.

On a day-to-day basis, you may sometimes get away with ignoring, avoiding or keeping to a minimum any interaction with people of other races. But when you do your volunteer work, the classroom-like education begins. It is different when you start seeing them regularly, talking to them and working with them on a regular basis.

You can also choose to volunteer with an organization that is predominated by people of your own color. Is that bad? Certainly not.

In the beginning, when you honestly feel that you need time to learn to live with other races, then you might be better off volunteering with that organization whose cultural affiliation you will better understand or cope with faster. It is always good to take things slowly, but surely.

Nevertheless, it would be a disservice to yourself if you will not strive to blend yourself with the reality that, if you intend to stay as an immigrant, people of other nations will be your neighbours, co-workers, church-mates, classmates or perhaps even your life partner.

1. *Consider volunteering a serious commitment. Thus, find a good reason for you to look forward to doing your volunteer work.*
2. *Volunteer for work that interests you and that will make good use of your talents and skills.*
3. *It is inevitable to meet people of various colors or persuasions in volunteer work. Welcome it as an opportunity to learn, understand, and blend with other cultures.*

10.3   So, How's Your English?

> IN THE WORKPLACE, ENGLISH IS GENERALLY THE ONLY ACCEPTABLE MEDIUM OF BUSINESS COMMUNICATION. BECAUSE OF DIVERSITY, MANY TIMES, YOU NEED TO BE A GOOD LISTENER MUCH MORE THAN A GOOD SPEAKER OF THIS LANGUAGE.

The first time I encountered having to be asked to certify my English proficiency was during the processing of my immigrant application. Knowing myself, I thought that I would be able to prove my English proficiency without having to go through a review class and examination which in my country cost a lot of money. I was not about to pay for something I knew I could do well.

I was educated in English-instructed schools and worked in large financial institutions where English was the medium of business communication. I had both bachelor's and master's degrees in communications. I edited magazines in English both in school and in my first job immediately after graduation from the university.

Upon arriving in Canada, the school principal that interviewed me for my child's transfer noticed my good English and thought that we had been staying in Canada for quite a while to be able to have the right accent. The truth was that we had only been there a week. Even when my child was asked to read an English book, the principal noticed how good her English was.

I wished it were that easy to be spoken to and carry out a conversation. But as we were coming along, I began to see the many versions of conversational English that I had to adapt to in order to be understood and to understand others. Remember, this is the land of many nations. The way people have learned and once spoke English back home is as diverse as their origins.

That is not a question for those who were born, grew up, and were educated in Canada. The English learned is spoken in more or less the same accent and intonation. That is English version No.1. The other conversational English versions are, as I said, as many as there are nationalities in the country.

This must be the reason why there is a class called Accent Reduction Course. It is intended to help the new immigrant re-train his tongue in order to adapt to the manner of speaking among locals. While it is not free, the course fee is not too stiff. Also, over time, you should be able to adjust your tongue and your ears as to how people speak the language.

The course that can be taken for free by adult learners is the English as a Second Language course, or ESL. This is offered in community centers, school boards and by some non-profit organizations. It is not so important that you know your English grammar perfectly as that you speak it well enough so you can be understood and you can understand people.

Many people who volunteer find their volunteer workplace as a good training ground to improve their conversational English. But whether it is in the real workplace or in your volunteer workplace, the work setting is where you will unavoidably meet and talk to people of varied languages. Yet, the only polite way to talk is to talk in English because it is supposed to be everybody's language of communication. When you find somebody at work who talks in the same dialect as you do, you should refrain from conversing in your own dialect when at work because that is being inconsiderate, if not impolite.

Often, it does not seem easy or even possible to change the accent or the intonation pattern. Thus, you have to be a good listener more than a good speaker. Although it is expected that you may have to ask the other person to repeat what has been said, it definitely is not all right to ask him to do that all the time, or at every sentence. But, no matter the consequences, it is better be safe than sorry, so ask to clarify the statement if necessary.

1. *Knowledge of the English language would not be a key criterion in your immigrant application if it were not important for your easy integration.*
2. *The spoken version of the English language is as diverse as the number of nationalities in a multicultural nation, so it is more important to be a good listener than a good speaker.*
3. *Unless you are in a writing or communications job, you should be able to adjust your conversational English to one that can be understood, especially in the workplace, including your volunteer workplace.*

10.4   How Much Time Should You Spend Volunteering?

> TREAT YOUR VOLUNTEER WORK AS IF IT IS YOUR FIRST JOB. YOU HAVE SO MUCH TO GIVE, YET YOU HAVE SO MUCH TO LEARN.

I can say I practically spent my first year in Canada doing unpaid jobs or volunteering. This was not because I could afford to not work, but for three reasons:

One, I wanted to focus on breaking in my family to the new life. I was initially bringing three children who came from a pampered life in my home country, not so much in the material sense, but regarding helping out around the house. Labour was cheap there and in abundance, so they grew up with nannies from birth.

Two, I myself did not know what I wanted to be. I had years and years of professional experience behind me. I had also a long list of things I wanted to do that I was not able to do in my past life. So, I felt I just had to coast along, go with the flow and discover what was best for me.

Three, I did not know many people when I came here. I had a friend of twenty years or so and her family and two more acquaintances from a past job. That's all. There had to be a way through which I could increase my network and spread myself, not specifically for a job, but simply to feel at home and welcomed.

I should say I was fortunate that I had enough allowance to sustain us through the first year but similarly, I also feel fortunate that I was able to go without work for a year because I was able to gather enough pebbles with which I am now building my foundation to a more enlightened and well-grounded future as an immigrant.

During that year, I was doing at least three volunteer works for three different institutions. I kept myself so busy that my family was chiding me about being even busier than any other person who has a fulltime job. I had meetings and duties even on weekends, with matching take-home assignments to submit to my group leader.

However, my case is probably more of an exception than the rule. I had so many lines of interest and so many perceived needs that I went along. And best or worst of all, I did not know what I really wanted or what I wanted to do first.

Ordinarily, I would think it is best to be able to choose one organization where you can concentrate your time and your effort especially if you do not have much to spare, or if you are already working. It is not good to spread yourself too thin, and in the process not being able to make a mark or to give your best shot. You still remember, of course, that the jack of all trades is master of none. The other wise man says, do not eat more than you could chew.

Even if you are not yet working, one or two volunteer jobs will be enough so that you can showcase your skills. It is not bad to admit that you are in that volunteer job to be discovered for your talents. But if you have too many commitments and foul up, instead of gaining the admiration of your co-volunteers or leaders, you might end up ruining your reputation.

Treat your volunteer work as if it were a job. If you are committed to do it on a certain day of the week, at a certain time of the day, do that with perseverance and reliability. If you have been assigned to do something, give it your best and do it with joy. Many times, those things that we do without consideration of money are things that bring out the best in us and give us the most happiness.

If I may have to go back to one of my thoughts earlier on volunteerism—it is to me an act of nobility and charity. Any such act must be treated with love and patience. This genuine desire to share your talent and time will radiate in your everyday encounter with people in the group and will show in the quality of work that you turn in.

1. *Your volunteer work may be the first "job" you might get as you start out a new life in your new country.*
2. *In it, you will have the opportunity to showcase your skills and gain the respect of other people.*
3. *So, the only rule is once you commit yourself and a portion of time to a volunteer work, strive to persevere, and prove to be reliable.*

10.5   What Is the Reward of Charity?

VOLUNTEERISM IS AN ENABLER. A NEW IMMIGRANT PARTICIPATES IN A PROCESS THAT ENABLES HIM TO DO GOOD TO HIMSELF AND ACHIEVE POSITIVE TRANSFORMATION BY THE VERY USE OF HIS OWN TALENTS AND SKILLS.

If I were uncomfortable about viewing volunteerism as a strategy to find work, the more I am uneasy about thinking of it is as being charitable and expecting any reward in return. But of course, my word has no bearing on the law of nature—what comes around, goes around, as I have said earlier. What you sow is what you reap. If you reap goodness, you will certainly sow goodness. Besides, volunteering is not necessarily viewed in Canada as simply a charitable act.

The issue of migration and migrants' integration in society in Canada has expanded the definition of volunteer work as being an ENABLER. It is a way for new immigrants to familiarize themselves with their new environment, mix with other people and re-engineer their skills and attributes in sync with the realities and needs of their community on the one hand, and their future workplaces on the other hand.

Volunteer work enables new immigrants to slowly but surely blend with the social, cultural, economic and even political tableaus of their newfound country. In a volunteer work at the early stage of his integration, the new immigrant thus becomes an instrument of his own adaptability and transformation.

Since he is not being paid and he contributes his time and talent with no material benefit whatsoever, he is developed into a new individual with his own dignity intact. He can take pride that such a transformation was mainly through his own initiative, his own decision to submit himself to a learning process. This is a process to which he mainly contributes what he brings with him—time, talent, skill, energy, enthusiasm, commitment—as capital, and from which he happily takes on whatever is taught to him or whatever he can gather in the process.

So, even if you want to call Volunteerism an act of charity, the net effect is in reality an act of charity to oneself. *To do volunteer work is to enable yourself to hasten and perfect your own ability to integrate in your new society.*

Yet, nothing can be more beautiful than being able to achieve that, while at the same time knowing your volunteer work indeed also help the organization and your community in many ways. Because volunteer work is usually undertaken in tandem or harmony with other people in your community, the whole benefit of the process goes around and brings positive results to everybody.

1. *Volunteerism enables the individual to hasten his integration into his new society.*
2. *Through volunteer work, the new immigrant becomes an instrument of his own adaptability and transformation, and thus reaps his own reward.*
3. *He is met with new challenges and difficulties in a semblance of a work setting, with his own dignity intact because he is not being paid and he has done so out of his own initiative to learn, to change and re-engineer himself.*

CHAPTER 11　　　NOW, YOU ARE READY
##　　　　　　　　　　FOR THE JOB SEARCH

11.1　　　**Which Job Search Help Organization Is Right for you?**

> NO JOB SEARCH ORGANIZATION WILL BE GOOD ENOUGH
> FOR A JOBSEEKER WHO DOES NOT PERSEVERE. ALL OF
> THESE ORGANIZATIONS WANT TO HELP, BUT IN THE END,
> ONLY YOU CAN BEST HELP YOURSELF.

Pretty soon, as you start assimilating the immigrant's life, you will realize that the host government really tries to make migration a sound business proposition. This is not to make money out of those coming in, but to prove that the country applies serious effort to make anybody's immigration decision worth its while.

Packing your bags and uprooting your family are major decisions. There should be enough reasons to say to yourself "I can make this work." That is where all sorts of government or government-funded programs come in to extend the best assistance to new immigrants to start a life and succeed in it in the long term.

The many years that Canada, for example, has been following this massive immigration program have given room for the birth of quite a number of non-profit, government-funded institutions or private organizations offering assistance to one's job search. For this book to fail to mention one or two of them or attempt to critique any of them would be a disservice to the great efforts they all put into their unitary mission.

These groups' biggest asset, I think, lies in the genuineness of their staff. Having been warmly welcomed and all, from them, you are bound to discover that kindness and good people still abound and are just waiting for us to discover and claim for ourselves.

These different organizations may compete for names for statistics because as in any government-funded organization, they need clients and good programs to continue to get support from government or to raise their own funds. Nevertheless, I believe that beyond the mission and vision that ensure them of funding, many of these organizations have evolved into a loving community of people working together to welcome the newcomers and bring fulfillment of dreams.

You as a client may start off as a mere number, but to me, how you convert yourself from plain statistics into a success story is pretty much a result of your own hard work and willingness to be helped in the process.

As you get acquainted with these organizations, it may not always be a rose-colored relationship through and through, and there could be some disappointments in the process. Be that as it may, to me what matters most is the sincerity of each group to help immigrants prepare for a new life and get them back into the workforce.

It is getting the client into the workforce that presents the biggest challenge. Curiously enough, only a few of these organizations include job placement as a direct service. But yes, they do have bulletin boards or job alerts for you. And I would say that being able to help you get a job also depends on the quality of their staff.

Based on my personal experience, if the help organization employees have genuine concern for each client, these employees go out of their own way to give tips and referrals for their clients even if that may not be part of their job description. That to me, is awesome, simply awesome. In my first year in Canada, I signed in with at least four of these organizations. I was told during my time that you may enlist with more than one organization for different programs but you cannot be enlisted in any two at the same time for a job search case management relationship. You are "owned" by an organization for at least 90 days before you can transfer to another one. Hopping to another organization is something you do sometimes when you want to fast-track your job search. But it did not matter to me that much because, luckily for me, I was not in such a hurry to get a job for at least one year. I was just happily rolling with the punches.

But how do you really choose the fairest of them all?

You don't.

There is no organization good enough to help you if you do not have the strength of character to persevere to get yourself into the workforce. May I refer again to my classmate-friend who, after having only landed for two weeks, got her first job and then an even better one after another six weeks. And I asked her, how did she do it? As soon as she affiliated herself with one of these organizations, she wasted no time and effort following up and asking them for tips and leads. She seriously persevered.

1. *Migration is such a serious mission in a country like Canada that job search help organizations abound.*
2. *These organizations may compete for your name to use for their statistics, but it is really up to you how to convert your own statistics into a success story.*
3. *Only those who seriously persevere in their job search make it ahead of their own timetable, with assistance from these organizations.*

11.2   When Was the Last Time You Wrote a Resume?

IT IS SO AMAZING HOW RESUME WRITING CAN BE SO MUCH AN ART, EVEN A SCIENCE, IN THIS JOB HUNTING JUNGLE. YET, THE SIMPLEST WRITTEN RESUME CAN BE THE KEY TO THAT FIRST JOB OPPORTUNITY.

Everything starts with a resume. Chances are, you have not written a resume in a long, long time. This is why the better question to ask is: Do you remember having written a resume?

Certainly, you have written a resume. But in a very competitive job jungle, the resume that you wrote long ago or even have recently rewritten will not stand much of a chance to be read at all. I never realized that there could be so many lessons to learn and techniques to acquire in writing even the simplest resume. To even more of my amazement, I never knew that anybody can have at least 50-100 versions of his own resume all at one time at the same time.

This book will not attempt to teach you how to write a good resume because, again, there are thousands of books and articles that can teach you that and hundreds of organizations willing to take you on to "case-manage" and help you with your resume. Yes, the exact term is case-manage. When you come in to one of these organizations, you are given a case manager and your name entered into a central database. Case management includes teaching you how to do your resume.

Up to this writing, I still could not pinpoint which of my resume versions was the best and guaranteed me a job. It turns out that the shortest and simplest one I wrote got me my first job. The resume version that got me my second job was the one I so quickly put together because in thirty minutes I had to leave the house to be able to get to the company's recruitment venue on time.

It was not because I was brilliant that I did that. The key is to be able to have a Word file of your core competencies and for each of these competencies, a maximum five-point enumeration of your transferrable skills. Depending on the position you are applying for, you pick from your tree of skills, and plant them into your resume. In that way, you will be able to do your appropriate resume version as fast and as customized every time you need one.

They say that your resume has only fifteen seconds of a reviewer's time to be read. In that case, even a standard two-page resume may not even be lucky to be read to the bottom of the first page. This is why, resume experts advise that you should be able to summarize both your skills and attributes in a maximum of seven bullet points at the top of your first page, with the heading Profile Summary or Summary of Skills and Attributes at the top of the page.

You may even need to omit the usual first heading Objective where you actually just type in the position applied for because that will even take two-three seconds of his fifteen seconds. Such Profile Summary may be the only portion that is read and right then and there, a decision is quickly made whether to proceed to the subsequent headings and information. You may have the chance to hop from one job search organization to another just as I did, with four different ones in the twelve months that I was trying to look for a job, albeit not so hard and seriously, as I mentioned before. But you will realize as I did that each of them will teach a different format, a new strategy, or a totally unheard of technique for doing that resume and getting it noticed, including a way to hide your age if you are re-entering the workforce as a second career or a comeback star.

But after four job search programs and twelve months of feeling my way around the job market, I would say there is no real guarantee except when you start to make up your mind and focus on what you want to do, or how you want to proceed with your job search. The least expected version of your resume may be the one that will get you your first job.

1. *When you move to a new country, you will realize how important a well-composed resume is in the job jungle.*
2. *Yet, there is no hard and fast rule in writing a good one except perhaps that you should be able to capture the reviewer's attention within fifteen seconds from the moment he picks up your resume to read.*
3. *Only when you start to focus on the fact that you need to get a job will even the simplest version of your resume guarantee getting you back into the workforce.*

A COVER LETTER IS AN INTRODUCTION TO YOUR RESUME.
IT MUST COMPEL THE REVIEWER TO GRAB A COPY OF
YOUR RESUME. BUT AT BEST, THE COVER LETTER MUST
GET YOU AN INTERVIEW WHETHER OR NOT THE REVIEWER
HAS READ YOUR RESUME.

My worst mistake in writing a cover letter was believing that there should be a standard cover letter, meaning that there is a standard format even in a cover letter.

Again, the cover letters that gave me my first two interviews are those that I wrote deviating from the standard format taught to me in my resume writing class.

The cover letter I was taught in one of the first job search organizations I attended was not necessarily bad or incorrect. The length was just right (keep it as a one-pager), make mention of the position you are applying for, summarize your skills, highlight your attributes, and close with anticipation.

Remember that the cover letter is intended to whet the reviewer's appetite to make him reach out for your resume. They say most reviewers get only as far as your cover letter. Failure to interest them at all with your cover letter is failure to invite them to view your resume.

If you are replying to an internet or electronic posting, both your cover letter and resume may not even catch the attention of the reviewer. So let me share with you a tip—make your cover letter your transmittal letter in your email message. Copy and paste the whole cover letter into your email. That guarantees that the cover letter gets through the first base of the elimination process. And if is written well enough, then lucky you, your documents may be set aside for further review.

But I want you to put in mind that the only objective of the cover letter is to get you an interview. Such being, you should be able to express your desire to be invited to an interview in a very subtle but expedient manner. Like, will they be missing a lot if they are not able to let you come in for an interview? Yes? Why not? But as I said, tell them in a very subtle manner, but not too coy. Be aggressive, but not abrasive. Write with a sense of urgency, but do not be imposing.

Certainly, already there are hundreds of books and articles that will tell you how to write your cover letter better or best. I am not about to compete with them. I just wanted to say here that the only kind of cover letter that worked for me was the one which I had written from the heart. Writing my cover letter from the heart was easy for those job postings that I feel strongly about, those that I was very much interested in because I firmly believed that I was best fitted for the position being advertised. In these, I was able to express what I had in mind, how I envisioned myself in this job, and how my interests and background could bring value to the position.

However, I was very careful about saying too much, too soon. First the reviewer might think it was too good to be true. Second, I might overvalue myself, and end up being perceived as overqualified. Third and most important, I might make the reviewer feel that I was a threat to his job or to his beloved boss.

The human factor is inevitable even in a cold-blooded job of having to review the one-thousandth resume coming in for a job posting. Anybody that reads a cover letter also reads in-between sentences and grasps unspoken messages. So while as the cover letter writer you want to be as natural and honest as possible, you are also compelled to think from the point of view of the person or persons who will review your application.

1. *A well-written cover letter is half the battle won to get a reviewer want to see you for an interview.*
2. *Thus, make sure that your cover letter covers the most salient points in your resume, and provides an interesting narration of your most valuable attributes.*

3. **Write a cover letter from the heart by being truthful. But do not discount the human side of the letter reviewer whose first impression of you in this letter will spell so much difference in getting you through the next steps.**

11.4   Can You Please Describe Yourself?

> YOU CAN ALWAYS TURN AN INTERVIEW TO YOUR FAVOR IF YOU DO YOUR HOMEWORK. WHILE PRACTICE MAKES PERFECT, NOTHING BEATS KNOWING YOURSELF AND HOW YOU FIT INTO THE JOB YOU ARE APPLYING FOR.

So your cover letter was good. Your resume successfully found its way into the hands of the right person. You are now on your way to an interview.

I am not a very fatalistic individual, but how many of us have such interesting stories to tell about that first job interview falling into our laps like it were falling down from heaven? Whether or not those were the circumstances, that in that first job interview, there is 101% chance that the first question that will be thrown at us is: *Can You Please Describe Yourself?*

If you are caught off-balanced by this very question, pardon me, but I think you are not ready in any way to go back into the workforce. It is as basic as eating three square meals a day, taking a bath, or going to sleep. After all, I already said that there is 101% chance that you would be asked to respond to this.

If you are in the job search game, by this time, you should already have the answer framed in your mind. Certainly, you can have 101 versions of that, too, because there is 101 job descriptions that you will want to respond to. Yet, just like in a cover letter or a resume, there is also standard information that an interviewer will look for in your WAP.

WAP is your self-introduction spiel or script. It should contain information on your **W**ork experience and relevant training, your **A**ttributes, and your **Passion**. WAP should be 90% **W**, 5% **A** and 5% **P**. Ideally, you should be able to recite it in a maximum of sixty seconds.

WAP is something you should have framed and memorized so that at any given time that someone winds the key, you can almost automatically recite the one appropriate for the "occasion." Yes, you just might be compelled to "recite" it in a very casual way, of course, to somebody you meet in an unexpected place. I did it more than a couple of times to some people I met at a Christmas store I did part-time work for. They asked me for a background on what I used to do, obviously a bit impressed at the smartness of how I handled my little job at the store.

Your local bookstore and the internet abound with hundreds of possible questions that could be asked of you in an interview. Then, of course, there's how to dress up or groom for the much-coveted interview session. But in a workshop I attended in one of Vancouver's help organizations, we were reminded that there were three significant questions which I think we should really be careful about:

One, is when you feel that you are being asked an "illegal" question. "Illegal" questions are those that may relate to your ethnicity, age, marital status, religion, disability or even gender orientation. One of the best responses to this type of question is "I'd be happy to answer the question, but may I know how it is related to the position I am applying for or requirements of the job I am applying for?" Or, "Sure, I'd like to answer that question but can you please tell the reason for asking?" Or, "Is this information necessary for me to be considered for the job?" Say these responses in the most polite way you can, never with a hint of being abrasive or irritated at all.

The key is to make sure you do not open the door for these illegal questions by saying too much in answer to a question. That includes not talking "aside" about your personal likes or dislikes or other circumstances that are not relevant to the job.

Two, know the answer to the question, "Will you be willing to relocate?" The truth is, most of us do not want to relocate, especially if you have just moved or landed in your host country. But it is best that you don't reply in the negative at once. One good answer is— "I can consider it, if a good opportunity presents itself."

Three, know how to respond to the question on salary expectation. The question does not pop up unless the prospective employer is about ready to decide that he wants you, usually at the second-level interview. But your reply to this can make or break the interview process that has worked to your favour. The first possible scenario is for you to try to evade the question by replying "I am flexible, but can we discuss it when we are both sure that I am the right fit for the job?" Or, say "I believe I shall be ready with my reply once I get full briefing on the duties and responsibilities expected of the position."

Even if you badly need the job, never say "yes" on the spot if you are quoted a price and you sense that you have the ace up your sleeve. Say, "May I let you know by the end of work day tomorrow or by (specify a work day, like Wednesday)?" It is best to give yourself at least 48 hours to keep to your excitement. The other caution is never to accept over-the-phone offer. Always go in only after you make final negotiations on the parameters of the job.

So, while we are on the subject of compensation, almost always when negotiating for a salary, a counter-offer usually will not exceed 20% of the original offer. However, it can also go anywhere higher depending on how urgent the need is for you or how you have been successful at convincing your interviewer that you are badly needed by the company.

There is also another way to gain advantage in the negotiation even if the counter-offer was not made or was way below your expectation. You can ask about or negotiate in terms of the perks or other benefits. When we were doing this exercise at the workshop, I was awed at how creatively but realistically those benefits can actually be, like bus passes, gym privileges, discounts or gift cards, daycare centers for kids or elderly, a cell phone or laptop, a company car, gas coupons, hockey tickets, flex time, shorter or fixed working hours, clothing allowance, housing or car loan, a grocery allowance, meal tickets, skills upgrading, workplace nap time, relocation allowance, paid sick days, internet cards, a parking allowance, a housing or rent subsidy, referral fees, birthday leave, association dues, and subscription fees. And more, as far as one's imagination goes.

It is very important that you exude self-confidence when you get to this point of the interview. Do your homework. Research on salary or pay scale for your position or the job you are applying for so that you will have a concrete idea of what it is you are negotiating for. Again, use your search engine. That is all on the internet. Or, you can ask some friends in the same line of work.

Another point I wish to emphasize before we leave this subject is being able to go around negative questions asked of you. For example, if you are asked to describe your best supervisor as well as your worst supervisor. I like what was taught to us in my workshop. First, describe the qualities of your best supervisor and then, proceed to simply say, "And my worst supervisor would be somebody who does not share the qualities of my best supervisor." In so saying, you do not put yourself into a situation where you need to talk against or negatively about anybody.

Most interviewers will pose situational questions and ask you what you would do about them. For example, "Can you think of a time when you had been given an impossible deadline and how did you handle it?" Whatever, situation question asked of you, remember the STAR formula.

S for Situation, describe it briefly. **T** for Task, what were you expected to do. **A** for Action, how you handled the situation. And **R** for Result, describe how the situation was resolved to the benefit of the company.

You sense an interview coming to an end when the interviewer turns to you and asks whether you wanted to ask something. Do not refuse to ask your questions. But to be safe, limit them to questions like: When will they be able to inform you of the result of the interview? Is it OK to call or email to follow up on the status of the application?

Sending a thank you card or email message to your interviewer immediately after the interview will work to your favour in terms of exuding courtesy and professionalism. That same thank you note or message may also serve to clarify some of your answers in the last interview and as a last sales pitch to your skills and qualifications.

1. *Interviews can be scary, but not if you come prepared.*
2. *Practice makes perfect, but how you describe yourself and your fit for the job will show how well you did your homework.*
3. *Stay positive all throughout, refuse to be intimidated, and express thanks for the time of the interviewer immediately after the interview.*

11.5   How Much of the Available Jobs Don't You See?

> THE HIDDEN JOB MARKET IS ONLY HIDDEN FOR THOSE WHO ARE NOT RESOURCEFUL, PERSISTENT AND PERSEVERING.

The fact that there is a hidden job market is no longer hidden.

It just means that, as a job seeker, do not waste your time on advertised jobs because they only represents 20% of the jobs available out there. 80% are in the so-called hidden market.

That also means that if 80% of the jobs are in the hidden market, 80% of your time should also be spent looking for these hidden jobs. Meaning, if you spend ten hours a day looking for a job, only two hours should be spent checking out internet or website postings or newspaper advertisements and similar public announcements. Eight hours should be used going out, meeting people, calling contacts or companies, walking in, and store-hopping.

It is not uncommon to hear stories of people having sent no less than fifty to one hundred resumes in short periods of time to internet or website postings but never getting any feedback except that standard reply of "Your resume has been successfully received. But only those being considered will be contacted, etc." The other frustration is with that fifty to one hundred resumes sent also came fifty to one hundred times you will have had to re-work your resume to fit the job being described in the posting. I, myself, probably have more than one hundred resume versions saved in Word.

So, what's the point of these companies blasting a posting in these virtual sites when they do not seem to have the time and the resources anyway to respectfully review each and every resume patiently sent to them by the poor jobseekers? Is it because they really just think it is the way of the future to do recruitment or to delist candidates? I bet the hard times even make matters worse for these companies who anticipate a deluge of resumes whenever they advertise or list a job online.

The other issue being raised here is the fact that some companies, even large and respectable ones, simply list jobs online in the name of non-discriminatory policy. But in reality, the positions are just ready to be filled up from within, if not already filled up. It is something verifiable, but who will admit it anyway?

On the other hand, from the point of view of the employer, I see a few reasons in "hiding" the available job:

One, the company still prefers to promote people from within their ranks, which is not really bad. Charity begins at home, so to speak.

Two, the company saves the trouble of having to interview hundreds for only one available position.

Three, the company feels safer to get names of possible candidates from more reliable sources like their own officers or employees, saving them the need to do more intensive background or reference checking.

Four, the company saves on the cost of advertising for the job available. Five, the need is urgent that word-of-mouth or putting it up within its own premises would be faster than having to produce an announcement material and having it published elsewhere.

These reasons should now give us an idea as to where to look for these hidden jobs. Thus, they also give us an idea on how to apply for them. I still insist that whether it is in the hidden or the open market, the job seeker needs to exercise some form of creativity and a lot of resourcefulness whenever a job is announced. A perfect example is working deeper on an internet posting by surfing on the company name indicated, getting the company number under Contact Us, verifying if the job listed is still available, asking if a drop-in resume can be accepted, getting the name of the manager whose department is involved in the posting and emailing your resume to this manager and not to HR, or actually visiting the company offices to leave your resume.

In the end, there is no such thing as the hidden job market when you know what you want, what companies you wish to work for, where you are able to spread yourself, when you spend time to go out of your shell and start not believing 100% what you see in the virtual sources. This is not to discount the fact that there are also great stories of jobs matched and found via these virtual sites, but I am wont to believe that they are better considered the exception and not the rule.

1. *It is good to be aware that 80% of available jobs in the market cannot be seen or read on a website or in an advertisement.*
2. *This being said, it is important that the job seeker spends just as much as 80% of his time looking for those hidden jobs.*
3. *Whether it is in the hidden or open job market, you need to be creative and resourceful. You also need to know what you really want, target companies you want to work for, and go out to find them.*

CHAPTER 12   WALK IN, WALK OUT

12.1   What is door-to-door selling?

> IF YOU HAVE LANDED FOR QUITE A WHILE AND STILL DO
> NOT HAVE A JOB, MOST PROBABLY, YOU HAVE NOT TRIED
> APPLYING DOOR-TO-DOOR.

In sales promotions, there is a technique called door-to-door. It is a selling technique where the seller literally knocks on the prospective customer's door to introduce the product and hope to close a sale.

The technique is usually off-the-shelf and can be used at any particular time and circumstances that the company sees necessary. It also depends on the kind of product or service that is sold, because not all can be literally peddled around. Thus, on the one hand, the technique easily caught popularity for products that you do not need to physically carry around, like insurance, investments and other intangible products or services.

I had been in marketing and did a lot of product promotions for quite a number of years in my past professional life. I have seen how different selling methods work for what, when, and how. I can distinguish which technique works for what, when and how. I can package products and make them attractive and more saleable. I can create a message, put it on board and spread it around to catch attention and eventually sell.

I was good at that. I was very good at that.

However, never in my whole life did I imagine having to sell myself door-to-door just to get my first local experience. Yet, I did it. But the saving grace is I did it not because my family was already starving, thank God, but because I was inspired and challenged by a good friend of mine who came to Canada and in less than two weeks was already working. She used door-to-door.

You want to know how effective it is? We talked about it on a Saturday night over dinner. The following day, Sunday, I went to a mall and in the third store that I entered, I got a job. And I applied for a job I never did in my entire life. Was I just lucky?

Lucky or not, there is no substitute from being able to get a chance to meet your prospective interviewer and employer right at first meeting. It may take you a hundred emailed resumes before you can even get to hear from, much less see, one right person from a company you wish to apply with.

Being at the right place at the right time? Perhaps. But how can you be in the right place if you do not go? And how can you be in the right time, when you are not there?

Mine and my friend's stories are definitely not the only amazing success stories of job hunting using door-to-door technique. A classmate in a seminar got a job on the second day of his landing. He went to a store and handed in his resume. He was told that they found him overqualified for the job. He looked at the store manager in the eye and said "I have just arrived. I do not have much money to spare and I have a family to feed." Can you do that if you faxed or emailed your resume?

We are, of course, talking about jobs here, and not yet a career. But who knows how many successful careers out there started with a door-to-door, give-me–any-job approach? Or just how you could stumble what has fate designed for you if you did not go out looking for it and spoke bravely of what you need and what you can do for a living?

Or how the self-confidence and strength of character were restored with one successful job search by knocking on an employer's door? That was what door-to-door did for me.

Talk about your chance to stand up in front of a prospective employer, speak for yourself and convince him that he needs you there, and right now. Only the door-to-door technique will do this for you upfront.

1. *Going door-to-door selling yourself may be something you haven't tried before, but it can be fun and rewarding.*
2. *Trying door-to-door may give you the satisfaction of being able to talk to a prospective employer on the spot, which may seem to take forever if you just emailed a resume.*
3. *The door-to-door approach may get you a job, and not yet a career, but it can also open up avenues for you to find a new career path or go back to your own.*

12.2   Are You Fit to Walk?

> YOU CERTAINLY NEED THE STAMINA TO DO DOOR-TO-DOOR. BUILD UP ON IT, DO YOUR DTD, YOU WILL END UP GAINING STRONGER CARDIO.

If you had lived a sedentary life, or your last job buckled you all-day long in front of a computer, then migrating to a country like Canada should be quite a change of pace for you. That is, if you choose to move around commuting in buses or the skytrain. And this is the reason why backpacks and walking shoes are more popular here, as are body bags and runners.

My intelligent guess is that it may be a year or so before you could be lucky enough to get your almighty driver's license. So, the car may not have to be necessary until then. I took that in stride because I figured that one of the earliest lessons I learned coming here was to be patient. There are no shortcuts. You need to gather your victories one day at a time, especially in trying to get a driver's license. Thus, you will need to love taking the public transport.

You must have always heard the expression, "Oh, you miss the bus." It's not that you got lonely and longed to see the bus. It really means you were a minute or a few seconds short of getting to the stop and catching your bus. And you will know the feeling, especially when you see its tail or when you have tried to run or waved at it in desperation. You can be lucky if the driver sees you or has the heart to wait for you. Most of the time, they won't wait. The worst feeling is being in front of the door and the driver closes it on your face, and takes off. That happens. But no hurt feelings. Can you imagine if bus drivers waited for everybody who runs or waves? They would never be as efficient as they are now in meeting their schedules.

So, every time you hurry down or run after time to catch your bus, consider it a free session for your cardio. After all, the treadmill and an hour at the fitness gym is at least $5.00 per hour for drop-ins. If you are not yet employed, that $5.00 could mean one more round-trip bus fare. It will also buy you one-litre milk, a dozen fresh eggs, and one loaf of bread.

The whole point is—you need to stay fit when you do door-to-door. This is because door-to-door literally means walking to and fro, climbing up and down stairs or moving back and forth a street. It is literally walking in and walking out of a store, regardless of whether there is a Now Hiring sign or not, and asking if by any chance, they are looking for help at the store.

Again, apply your math: The more doors you knock on, the greater your chances are of hitting the jackpot. So, the more you are fit, the more energy or stamina you have to do this.

If you are doing door-to-door in a mall, the conditions are far better than when you were doing it downtown or in the streets. The advantage though of doing it downtown is the fact that head offices and HR departments are many times in the store's downtown locations. Nevertheless, store managers, even in malls, usually have authority to hire people for store duties, especially if it is for temporary or seasonal employment.

On the first week that you intend to do door-to-door, give your feet a gap of at least a day to rest. Certainly if you are not used to doing this before, you will want to break in yourself first. And your feet will tell that to you.

On the following week, do it two or three consecutive days to take advantage of your inertia at work. You will be better off too getting used to the "daily" walk or schedule than having to rest and then pick up again. Sometimes, our bodies just need breaking in and pretty soon, we will realize that they have adjusted to the pressure. And because you are still out of job and economizing, bring your water, cookies and candies to quench thirst and little hunger away.

To save energy and time, it is important that you plan your itinerary for the day as to which area or which stores in the area you want to walk in. This presupposes too that you have studied your map and your directions. There is nothing more frustrating than starting off with a place that you could not find and then grow weary in the process and not continue out of irritation.

1. *Stay fit and build up your stamina.*
2. *Because door-to-door literally means walking in and out of your target stores or offices, your legs and feet will take a beating and you will need to physically prepare for that.*
3. *Be really organized too in terms of your itinerary. Plan your walks and bring little provisions to satisfy thirst and hunger without dipping deeper into your not-yet-earning pockets or wallets.*

12.3　　　What Do You Say?

> "ARE YOU BY ANY CHANCE HIRING?" "OH YES, CAN YOU START TODAY?" THESE ARE POSSIBLE WORDS TO BE SPOKEN AND HEARD IN A DOOR-TO-DOOR.

When you do door-to-door at mall stores, for example, you are most likely to encounter sales staff or managers who are busy at work. This particular circumstance can work both ways for you. Either you are unable to penetrate at all because no one can entertain you at the moment, or you are able to penetrate too quickly because the store manager happens to be so pressured that he feels he needs help right then and right at that moment.

The second situation got me my first store job. As soon as I decided to get a store job and do door-to-door, I walked around a large mall. On my way to a third prospect, I read this catchy tagline to a store's name that said "Established Since 1871." With a little bit of wit and happy-go-lucky decision, I said to myself that this was the store where I should apply because it was more than a hundred years old and still going strong. I should be so lucky to get a "stable" employer.

When I went over to the cashier's counter and asked if by any chance they were hiring, she almost jumped off her cage to get me the manager. When the manager did not come out as she promised, this lady cashier brought me instead to their stockroom and introduced me to their store manager. I handed my resume, and the manager took it without even looking up because she was so busy wrapping orders. She asked me the magic question: Can you describe yourself? Whoa, my chance to recite my WAP!

My WAP was strictly short, just about six sentences. But before I could even get to the third sentence, she snapped back and said, "Oh, I'm sure you know how to deal with people. Can you start today?"

Those were perhaps, the most beautiful words I have ever heard since my torturous days of job hunting. It did not matter to me that I was taking on a job I had not tried in my entire life, yet here I was being given the chance to do. Excited that I was, I did not even ask how much I will be paid per hour. Silly me. I had to rush to send my son home who was then at the mall with me.

So, what do you say in a door-to-door application? If you are lucky to be entertained, you go up to the cashier to ask "Is it by any chance, you are hiring?" Or, "Are you hiring?" This is if there is no sign on the window that says "Now Hiring."

If she says "Yes," or "Oh, sure, hand in your resume," you must know by now the rules in modifying or customizing your resume to fit the job you are applying for. For a store job, give your version of the resume that will show your experience or skills at selling or dealing with customers, or your accounting, bookkeeping or cashiering background, or your purchasing, inventory management, or merchandising abilities.

Two things may happen: She will get your resume and tell you that you will be notified, or she will get your resume and usher you to the store manager. This is what I'm saying when I say that door-to-door gives you an opportunity to speak right up to your prospective employer, as store managers usually have authority to hire for their branches or outlets. This is a moment that you might have to wait for what feels like forever if you were only doing your application via the internet.

The interview session, thus, becomes instant and impromptu. But it should not be to you. We said, before going out there, you should have done your homework, wrote your WAP, reviewed the Most Asked Questions in interviews, noted all possible work situations that may be relevant to the job and composed answers in your mind as to how you had handled those situations.

Remember the technique that was taught to me in one of the workshops I attended? The STAR response method to any situation-based question? **S** is stating the Situation, **T** is for Task, **A** is for Action and **R** is for the result. The STAR formula ensures that you do not get tempted to give a self-serving answer to a situational question. Self-serving answers always leave a bad taste in the mouth. The STAR formula, however, guides you to keep your response as objective and as truthful as possible by focusing on the given Situation, your Task or your role in it, what Action you employed and what the Result of that action was.

It is important to state a result that will show how the team or the company benefited from your action or how you handled the situation. For example, Question: Describe one situation that tested your flexibility. Answer: There was an instance that I had to attend two meetings that conflicted in schedules because one was reset at the last minute

(Situation). While I needed to attend both meetings, I obviously could not be in two places at the same time **(Task)**. So I had to prioritize as to which meeting needed my physical presence, and since one meeting was going to discuss logistics, I asked an assistant officer who was good on administrative matters to attend the meeting instead **(Action)**. The result was we were fully updated on both meetings and the assistant officer was happy that she was trusted to sit in that meeting **(Result)**.

Whatever way you want to apply for a job, the lessons are the same, except may be that one is being done in a faster pace and more abbreviated form, as in a door-to-door technique.

In an on-the spot interview like this, conditions may be different as to the formality of the place, but you should keep your composure and always remain coherent. And since the interview may be more fast-paced and to the point, remember to say the most relevant information at the beginning and elaborate only when you have time. You may also be a little more aggressive given the urgency of the situation, but do not lose your grace and dignity, even if you will have to beg for a job to feed a family.

1. *A door-to-door application gives you the possibility of talking to your prospective employer on-the-spot.*
2. *Whether it is on-the-spot or a scheduled interview, remember your STAR formula when answering a situation-based question.*
3. *State the Situation, define your Task, relate the Action you took, and do not forget to relate the positive Results of that action.*

12.4   What Jobs Are Available Door-to-Door?

> YOU HAVE TO BE AWARE THAT THERE IS NO PROMISE OF LONG-TERM FUTURE IN A TEMPORARY OR SEASONAL JOB YOU GET DOOR-TO-DOOR. BUT THERE CERTAINLY IS A POSSIBILITY OF GETTING INTO A NEW CAREER PATH OR GOING BACK TO A CAREER IF YOU DO THIS WELL.

When we discuss this topic, we will refer more to the temporary or seasonal nature of the jobs. I will be citing retail store job only because it is nearest to my knowledge and experience at the time of this writing. But door-to-door can also mean one clinic to another, one travel company branch to another, one security agency to another, and so on.

Door-to-door literally means walking in and out of the doors of the type of company or employer that you want to apply for. I suppose we also do door-to-door to one which is has a semblance of relationship to our previous experiences. This, even if you get stuck with retail stores, you do door-to-door to pharmacy store if you used to be a pharmacist; an optical shop if you used to be an optician; a furniture and home decor store if you were an interior designer, and the like.

Obviously, when you walk, for example, from any store to store, the positions or work available are those that they do at the store—sales, cashiering, bookkeeping, records clerk, warehouseman, inventory clerk, and store manager. But since the hiring officer will most likely be the store manager, he is not about to hand his job over to you when you apply.

Let us be clear also that academically, when you are doing a door-to-door hunting, you are looking for a job, not a career or a chance to practice your profession. When I did my first store job, I was tempted to pity myself. Well, in fact, I have to admit, I cried in bed for two nights at least. But that was all.

This was because on my way home after my third day at the store, at the skytrain I was engaged into a conversation by another lady on her way home too. She was a sales assistant like myself, but she was a medical doctor by profession. From my country, I know how expensive and how difficult it is to become a doctor. Notwithstanding, how long, which is on the average eight to ten years of studying, residency and internship. While I was an assistant vice president from my past professional life, it did not cost me that much nor did it take me that long to prepare academically for my career. So why cry on the third day?

But do you believe in destiny?

Earlier I said, *where you are is your destiny. What you will be will be the result of what you do where you are.*

While you may be out looking for a store job, it can happen that you will get to meet some other people who will be instrumental in putting you in an entirely different job or another job. Your very act of walking in and out of these stores is networking in itself. In that, along the way, you may meet someone who will bring you what could have been designed for you.

You may call me fatalistic. But you cannot tell me now that it does not happen, because it does happen.

It can also happen that your store job may mean the start of an entirely new career path for you. You may have always known you were good with people and convincing people, but you never really tried selling to people. Suddenly, you discover that you enjoy meeting people from all walks of life at the store, helping them make choices, and sending them off happy and contented with your brand of service.

While I cried on my first two nights of my store job, I was also very delighted because there is unspeakable satisfaction and joy in being able to make customers happy. You feel good when they tell you that you are a good salesman, that you make good suggestions, that you are very attentive and helpful.

I even had husband-and-wife customers who had to hug me when they left the store because they were just too happy that I helped them out. Or the very thoughtful daughter who was buying a present for her Mom and went back a week after to introduce me to her Mom and told her that I was the lady who assisted her with her gift choice. Or the retired gentleman who had to apologize for changing his mind about a purchase but promised to buy something else next time because I had been warm and hospitable.

Never underestimate what a door-to-door job can do for you.

1. *Most jobs you will find available door-to-door will be temporary or seasonal.*
2. *Even if you are looking at it from this point of view, remember that the exposure and the experience will stay with you for all time.*
3. *Thus, do your best and gather as much learning and experience even in the most menial job. You will look back and will be happy that you did it.*

12.5   How Long Should You Stay in This Job?

> GOING DOOR-TO-DOOR GETS YOU A JOB, NOT NECESSARILY A CAREER. IF YOU WILL NOT FIND YOUR CAREER IN IT, MAKE SURE YOU LEAVE ENOUGH TIME FOR YOU TO LOOK FOR OTHER OPPORTUNITIES WHILE DOING IT.

Okay, I understand. No matter how happy that store job has made you, you are still stuck with a job and not a career. This is particularly an issue for those of us who are skilled in an entirely different profession and academic background.

But may I lovingly advise that the issue should be clear, that you simply want to go back to your career or own line of specialization. Why? Because if the issue is because you are ashamed of a job which you think is menial, then there is another problem that goes back to yourself. Even if you want to go back to your previous line or skill, starting from the ranks is more likely to happen than being able to get to your previous level at once. Meaning, you will start with menial tasks nevertheless.

If you have not made up your mind whether to go back to your old career or not, or want to go back and spend time looking for an opportunity there, then it will be wise to do part time or get into a seasonal employment.

Doing this part-time will allow you to have a window to continue looking for work that matches the skills you are bringing with you officially to your new country, and to upgrade these skills by enrolling in part-time courses.

But you will also find yourself really needing time to attend to family errands, household chores and personal concerns, because house helps may not be around to do them for you. Oh, that should make us miss the days when back home, we had all the help we could get to do things we could not or did not want to do.

A few weeks into your first store job, for example, see if you can be accommodated for more convenient hours of work or a schedule that is more attuned to your other concerns. I want you to do this very cautiously because you might end up losing the job. And when I say cautiously, I mean, study whether your role is important to the company, whether you have exhibited your reliability, whether the manager allows that, whether some employees do that, or whether you can state your case convincingly.

It depends on each of our circumstances, but I think that having to work two days straight for eight hours is better than working three days for six hours. The amount of effort you exert preparing for work and making arrangements for your family is definitely more taxing if you have to do it three days a week than if you were to do it only twice that week. Plus, the fact that this one extra week day can help you attend to errands that require you to call or visit people or offices on regular work days and hours is practical, isn't it?

Then, there is another set of people who may want just a job, and that's it. There is little concern for any career to build up or prepare for. And I am not saying that this is bad. This is only a statement of fact. This group may also want to take up two part-time jobs simultaneously, and certainly arrangements can be done to be able to do both, and most employers understand and accede to that. This is the reason why in most companies you will be asked to submit your Availability Hours on a fairly regular basis.

Availability Hours as a day-to-day or weekly SOP is acceptable in companies that take on part-timers and seasonal employees. It's not that these companies do not care about your professional growth, but only because they also recognize your more pressing need at that moment. Certainly, some of these companies offer part-time or seasonal employees full-time employment if these workers had been able to exhibit their reliability and skills very well.

This brings us to the issue of being able to give your best all the time, regardless of the type or nature of your employment with any company. I have always believed myself and this I tell my fellow workers, "If you're good, you're good." It will show and you will shine. And it will be your key to anything better in the future.

The other concern is the danger of complacency in working part-time jobs. It is not bad that we enjoy hopping from one job to another, or bicycling from one part-time job to another. But it is always better to always think long-term. There are disadvantages to this type of employment, and it is important that you recognize these disadvantages. We will discuss this in a later chapter.

1. *Temporary or seasonal jobs are mostly part-time.*
2. *You can do two part-time jobs at the same time but make sure you do not foul up on making your availability clear and reliable.*
3. *Think long-term, whether for the career that you still want to build or prepare for, or to this employer which you want to keep as your part-time source of bread and butter.*

CHAPTER 13   WARM-CALL, COLD-CALL

13.1   What Is the Use of That Phone Again?

> THE LOWLY TELEPHONE SITTING IN YOUR HOME CAN ACTUALLY BE YOUR VERY INSTRUMENT IN FINDING THAT ELUSIVE JOB.

One nice thing about writing is you are forced to read widely about everything so that your readers can learn from you. In the process, however, you are the one really learning and discovering things you thought you knew all along.

Until this topic, I did not know how much controversy was stirred by the very invention of the telephone instrument, including a real court battle among the protagonists. In the end, the world ended up recognizing Alexander Graham Bell as the inventor of the practical telephone, the one that made possible its mass production and later commercialization.

That was only because, according to a story, he (well, his lawyer) beat the other one on paying the filing fee with the patent office, even though the other one got to the office ahead of him by a few hours. Nevertheless, it was a long-running battle not only among the two, but with many other equally brilliant scientists and inventors who delve into this voice communications wonder.

That is to say that anything important cannot be rewarding if we do not go out of our way to beat ourselves to it. That spells the difference between brilliant and smart. It's not that you should outsmart anybody, but that you should be smart enough to think and act at least two steps ahead if there is something that you really, really want.

While technology has been so much revolutionized, with so many inventions that have made so many things so accessible and convenient to people, Bell's telephone takes credit for making possible that connection so fast while still being a bit personal.

In your job hunting, one of the fastest ways by which you can move a step closer to a prospective employer is through the use of the telephone. You can do it in the convenience of your home, with the convenience of your own time and at the convenience of your own budget, because it will not cost you any additional expense if you already have a landline anyway.

Yes, it is true. Sometimes, the most ignored assets are those which are nearest to us or closest to us, be those people or things. How many times do we plan or intend during the day to call a friend or call to inquire and never really do so? We forget, we procrastinate, we do something else, or we think that is easy because the phone is always there anyway. Yet, how many jobs have you missed do you think by not doing so?

Or, probably, we were afraid it was not really that easy to call anybody from out of nowhere or without having anything in common and tell your bit of story. Sorry, but I do not understand how you can brave a job interview if you cannot manage to make a warm call or a cold call. So, that keeps me wondering how you can ever find a job.

To differentiate, a warm call is making a call to somebody whom you may know from a reference or who may be expecting your call as a result of previous introductions or referrals. Making a warm call, I should say, should be more desirable and easy.

A cold call is calling from out of nowhere with no previous introduction at all to whoever will happen to take the call. It's more like a chance conversational encounter between two people, but with an element of deliberate will from the one who initiated the call because he has an agenda to take up. Cold calling may be understandably uncomfortable, but I guess the worst that you may get is a rejection to be connected to anybody (whom you do not know anyway).

Whether warm calling or cold calling, you will find that the telephone becomes your best friend because it is instrumental in creating the bridge between you and the possibility of being able to get a job or may lead to getting a job without even leaving the comfort of your home. Any failure or rejection does not cost you anything, as long as you managed your call right from your end.

1. *Befriend the phone that sits around your house. Use it to discover jobs in the hidden market.*
2. *Because the phone is always there, fight the tendency to procrastinate in making those important calls.*
3. *If you cannot manage to make a cold call, it may even be harder to face a job interview.*

13.2   How Do You Begin?

> YOU NEED A PLAN TO MAKE SURE YOU ARE STARTING OUT RIGHT IN THIS COLD CALLING TECHNIQUE.

It is human nature that we so believe in something because it has actually happened to us. I remember a job coach who was talking to us so animatedly about her faith in the power of cold calling because that was exactly how she got her current job. The testimony is stronger if spoken from the voice of successful experience and realistic encounter with the ideology.

While my lowest grade was in math, to me, the simple mathematics is going for as many techniques in job hunting as you can to give yourself you as many chances at succeeding. There's also believing that one plus one is not necessarily two. If you add one to one, you get more than two chances of being able to find a job.

But how do you really begin to make those calls?

As in anything, you need to plan out your course as if you are going on a road trip without hitting the road (because you only need to do it without leaving your place. Hmm, this looks a lot easier that door-to-door, feet-wise anyways).

Have you decided on what industry you wish to work for or try your luck for a start? Make a list of companies in that particular industry or industries that you intend to target. Do you want to hit the big time or go for the small ones?

There are at least two schools of thought in job hunting for beginners or new immigrants: The first is to hit the big time, and immediately go after your own line and level. The second is to try to find something else where you can start at an entry point, whether this in an industry you have worked for or not at all.

The first school of thought is sadly the one that is pounded on would-be immigrants in workshops in their own country as if it was easy and possible. Possible it may be, but .probable? Rarely. In fact, it's exceptional. And that is the reality. What, one out of ten or one out of a hundred, or one out of a thousand? Nobody has the correct statistics on his hands, but go and ask an immigrant on the street.

I went for school of thought No. 1. bravely for one year, because I had money to last me for one year or so without work.

But what was the first job I got? A store job. This is not to demean the job itself, but for a skilled professional, that was a challenge, a challenge not to fight the system, but to fight the fear of one day giving up and deciding to pack my bags and go back to my otherwise gorgeous life in my own country.

So, you begin by deciding between school of thought No. 1 and No. 2. If you do not have much to spare, the sooner you decide to embrace one school of thought, the better. Remember that the money you bring with you has been diminished even before you can even start spending it by the reality of foreign exchange rate system. Sticking to one school of thought does not need to be for as long as one year as I did. You can choose one for only two or three months or so, and then switch.

I will not prescribe which school of thought you should take up because the lessons are better learned and the successes are better gained when you have made decisions you believed in and are happy about them in the beginning. After all, there is no right or wrong school of thought. The difference lies in when you will chance upon your biggest break and how. Not how soon, only how.

Again, you should believe that many times the biggest success comes in very unexpected places and ways. Cold calling may be, yes, cold and drab, but the job that you may be the most happy about may be the one you get out of one of those cold calls you make, just like my job coach.

1. *It is always good to start out with a plan on how to proceed with your cold calling.*
2. *Ask yourself if you want to target the big companies at the outset, or if you want to start with the smaller companies to gain experience.*
3. *List the companies you want to work for and where you envision yourself to be working.*

13.3   Do You Have What It Takes to Make That Call?

COLD CALLING MIGHT NOT BE FOR EVERYBODY. THAT IS THE TRUTH. IT TAKES CERTAIN ATTRIBUTES TO BE ABLE TO SUCCEED IN IT.

Many times, one of the easiest things to procrastinate about is one that is within your very reach or resources. You sort of always say to yourself, oh, that is easy to do, I can do that anytime. As in cold calling, Oh, that should be so easy, the phone does not have a set of feet. It will stay right where it is. So, I can do my cold calling later.

It is a very simple task but it takes somebody with specific attributes to be successful in it. One must be Focused, Organized, Patient, Persistent, Smart, and Humble.

Focused. I am sure that, before you decided to come over, whether for reason of family or only yourself, you had many things going on in your mind as to the many possibilities that you could do once you are here. Probably, these are things you never had the chance to do while working full-time in your own country, or things you had started but never got around to finishing. But once you arrive, you will realize that there is really much, much more that you can delve into because the opportunities really just present themselves at your feet. You should be happy about this, of course. But it can also easily confuse you and make you lose focus. Suddenly you will not know what you want. You might want a lot and not know where to start or what step to take up first.

In a task as simple as trying a job hunting technique like cold calling, it is equally important to be focused on where you want to start at the very least. Make up your mind on the area or industry where you want to search for a job. If you have just landed, this could possibly be the area or discipline where you worked before. If you used to work in a bank, then you might want to start with financial institutions. If you used to work as an insurance advisor, then the insurance industry will be your first choice.

Organized. Being organized is an attribute that we all of course need to possess in almost all aspects of our lives. We should be organized both in our heads and in action. They say, if your first job is "to job hunt," then you should have an "office". And when you have an office, you should have a corner with a telephone. So that takes care of the physical side of organization.

You should also be organized as to your plan of action. Such a plan should have a neat list of companies that you have chosen to cold call. These companies should be so arranged as to which one you are most interested in. This, so that if you get positive result in the first ones on the list, you may not need spend time going to the others in the list.

Patient. The most difficult task is to do what we once thought was the easiest task, especially if it is too repetitive. We get easily irritated when what we thought was easy, turns out to be difficult after all. Or, we get impatient with ourselves if we cannot get through faster for something we thought we could do easily.

Cold calling tests our patience—dialling, getting a busy signal, getting the wrong number, being on hold for so long, not getting through the right person, getting screened too tightly, being rejected altogether. But count your blessings, not your sorrows. At least you are only seated on a comfortable chair at home. At least you can continue re-dialling without your feet getting sore. At least you do not see the face of the person screening or rejecting you. At least there is no additional cost to you if you redial or move on to another number.

Persistent. I believe only a person that is consistently persistent can get ahead of the others or maybe even ahead of his own timeline. When you do warm calling or cold calling, it is easy to fall prey to boredom and exasperation. Understandably, I do not know of anybody who derives pleasure in dialling or redialling, except maybe the call center agents who are paid well to do the job. Other than them, we only think of spending too much time on the phone as a waste.

Perhaps the key is to re-orient our thinking on that. Remember the parable of the persistent person who kept knocking at the judge's door until the judge woke up to talk to him and ask what he wanted. If you are doing cold calling, think of it as a job, like a job that you are being paid to do, only the pay or the rewards will come much later. If the person on the other line is about to reject your call or put you through, persist to get the right person on the line. This is where the smart you should work.

Smart. Not all brilliant people are smart. But smart people are certainly brilliant. I say that from the point of view that brilliance comes from the intellect. But the smart person can not only think well, but also can feel right about something. Being smart implies both social and emotional intelligence. It will take a smart person to outwit an efficient secretary or receptionist who refuses or cannot be easily persuaded to let you talk to somebody else in the company except herself, especially if she does not know you from Adam.

I do not want to use the word clever, but smartness and persistence put together will definitely give you headway and open up doors or communications for you. So it becomes all the more important to be very decisive on the companies that you really want to pursue because I do not think you want to waste those attributes on something you are not necessarily serious about. Then it may not be worth the effort.

Humble. This is the hard part, I suppose. For me, it was. Although in my heart I knew that for me to be able to start all over again in many facets of my new life, humility would be the only attribute that could pull me through. When you come from a gorgeous life earning big money, it can be extremely difficult to even think that the money you brought with you will be gone soon. In fact, sooner, if you do not muster enough humility to admit that life is totally different now and money might not come so easy if you do not get a job.

But the harder part of being humble is when you start getting instructions from people who cannot even complete a grammatical, error-free English sentence, or bossed around by someone who is a college dropout, or reprimanded by a fellow countryman for not mopping the floor well or not doing your door duty efficiently. But do not make the mistake of interchanging the word humble and the word stupid. The other school of thought is for you to learn to assert yourself given the right timing and circumstance. You at least owe that to your years of hard work building your reputation and character.

Humility in cold calling means that you address the other person on the line with due respect, regardless of position or rank he holds in the company he is working for. Remember, you are the caller and you are the one who needs a favour. The telephone operator, front desk clerk, or receptionist will be key to your getting through. So it is inevitable that you treat them like they hold your dear life in the palm of their hands, literally, with that call. Treat them respectfully and as an equal.

1. *Cold calling sounds so easy, anybody can do it. This is not necessarily so.*
2. *It takes specific human attributes to jumpstart and sustain cold calling, being Focused, Organized, Patient, Persistent, Smart, and Humble.*
3. *Never forget that in this technique, you are the caller and the one who needs help. Treat the other person on the line accordingly.*

13.4   Do You Know What to Say?

> WHAT YOU SAY IS AS IMPORTANT AS HOW YOU SAY IT.
> AS SOON AS SOMEONE PICKS UP THE PHONE, THE MOOD
> SHOULD BE UPBEAT AND FRIENDLY.

In any company, the first line of defence, if we may call it that, is the person who mans the entrance desk and or who holds the switchboard. That is, of course, the secretary-receptionist or the telephone operator. Some call them the gatekeepers.

When I thought that I was going to get a job as an office receptionist in Vancouver, I started to evaluate and internalize the "job description," trying very hard to call to mind what our frontliner at my previous office was doing or what we expected her to do for our company executives.

Among all other "related duties that may be assigned from time to time", the office receptionist or secretary is expected to screen calls and visits for the bosses. She must therefore be perceptive and smart enough to deliver her standard lines and make up credible excuses on behalf of the boss so that the latter may do his job without much interruption from people who can be saved for later attention or warrant none at all.

So it takes a smarter person to outsmart the smart secretary or receptionist. What you say is, therefore, important.

Perhaps it is significant at this point to mention that cold calling is actually an age-old selling technique, like door-to-door is. It's a salesman's tool.

We all agree, of course, that the good salesman certainly has a way with words and convincing people.

But did you know that even salesmen dread cold calling? There is something about cold calling that scares them, probably because cold calling is so much a leap into the unknown. Or maybe it's the fear of rejection or embarrassment.

Today, you may want to refer to cold calling as outbound telemarketing. Outbound telemarketing is tough. Even the best call center agents dread this job description. And for those who have no choice but to do it, the pay is better and a lot higher because of the nature of the function, which is most of the time sales. Since most of us are on the other side of the fence, the ones being called by telemarketers, we know how difficult it is to be talking to by somebody uninvited trying to sell us something. In fact, some actually refer to cold calling as the uninvited job hunting technique.

This fear is aggravated perhaps by the overstated objective of cold calling—to sell. It is quite ambitious to aim to close a sale from one cold call. But you could be lucky. I remember when an accident insurance telemarketer made a cold call to my home phone number, he hit the jackpot because I signed up for a plan with that call. Why? Just a day before I was involved in a car accident. Yet, how many times could you have such a coincidence?

Realistically, for a salesman, cold calling must simply aim for getting an appointment; and for a job hunter, to simply get the name of a contact who has relevant information on a job opening. As such, the opening statements must address those objectives.

Furthermore, as recognized earlier on how important the gatekeepers are, it is inevitable that we properly address their role in the exercise. Look at them as those that can help you, not as those that will hinder you from getting through.

"Hi, I wonder if you could help me . . ." could be a better opening greeting than saying, "Hi, my name is _____". After all, if he does not recognize the name, his first reaction will be to wrinkle his forehead, raise his eyebrows and dig deeper down into his brain trying to recall if he had met anybody by that name. In other words, the first reaction could be negative because you are unduly stressing them. But if you open by acknowledging that they could be of help to you, that should be flattering, right?

Have you realized that most of the time when you call a company, the opening greeting is "ABC company, how may I help you?" Thus, whether they mean it or not, the original intention is to be of help. So, to that greeting, you may respond by saying, "Hi, I need your help" or "Oh, yes, I need your help." If the other line's greeting is only, "ABC company, good morning", then say "Hi, I wonder if you could help me" or "Good morning, I need your help."

What you say next is even more important. Focus on the objective of your call. If this is your first call, target only being able to get a contact name, his exact designation, department name, and complete address. The contact name should be the name of the person in the company who can get you hired because he will find value in what you can offer. This is not the HR officer, but the head or assistant head of the department where you intend to be assigned when you work for the company.

But before you can ask for that, you should be able to say something relevant and convincing to be able to persuade the other person on the line to give you that information. This presumes that you have researched the company that you are calling. So after the greeting, you can say for example, "I have followed recent developments in your company, including your plans to tap the Asian market in Vancouver. I would like to submit a "proposal"" (I put proposal in quotes because you actually intend to propose that they give you a job or consider your skills to expand the company's business among Asians in Vancouver). Then say, "I need the name, position title and contact details of whoever heads the department that is in charge in market expansion or new market development."

In summary, the opening conversation could go like -

"ABC Company, good morning. Pam speaking, how may I help you?"
"Oh, hi Pam. I need your help. I have followed recent developments in your company, including your plans to tap the Asian market in Vancouver. I would like to submit a proposal. I need the name, position title and contact details of whoever heads the department that is in charge in market expansion or new market development."

The conversation could go anywhere from there, so you will need to envision the different scenarios that might take place after that introduction statements. In scenario one, Pam may ask for your name and other details. In scenario two she may be convinced and give the information you need. In scenario three, she may reject the idea of giving out names to a stranger. At this point, you should be able to try and draw some connection between you and ABC Company—you may be an existing client, you may be part of that Asian market, you may know somebody in that company, you may be very knowledgeable of the Asian market and can help them, etc. But try very hard to withhold the fact that you are applying for a job. That is not lying, just postponing telling your real agenda.

Remember that your short-term objective is to get the name of the person who can offer you a job. If you did your opening intros well, you might be able to get that. But the conversation can also cause the gatekeeper to be too accommodating and ask you if you want to speak to this person and go ahead to connect you. Don't panic. If you have prepared, then this is the moment of truth for this cold call. What do you say?

At this point you might need to introduce yourself and speak about how much you have read, for example, about the need of the company to explore and expand its operations towards the Asian market. Talk about your connections and experience with this market, including your eagerness to apply these to any possible chance to work with this company. Ask for an appointment to meet up with him so you can explore together how you can help them in this regard.

Then how do you end the call?

End your call with the beginning in mind. Get a contact name so you can write a customized letter addressed to this person, or a date for an appointment for a job interview or possibly a mere exploratory talk. Close with the most standard statement and yet, something you should never, never forget—thank you. Always thank the person for giving you time or help, like "Pam, thank you so much for your help. And have a nice day ahead of you."

1. *On a first call, stick to a minimum objective: Get the name and contact details of the hiring manager, not the HR manager. The hiring manager is the head of the department you might wish to join.*
2. *The next step after a successful cold call is to be able to write a more customized letter introducing your skills and how you can help the unit achieve its business goals or expand operations, as the case may be.*
3. *Always end your call noting attainment of the minimum objective you have, and with a sincere thank you for the help of the other person on the line.*

13.5   So, What Is Cold Calling Again?

> COLD CALLING IS UNINVITED JOB HUNTING. LIKE AN OUTBOUND TELEMARKETER, YOU ARE ACTUALLY LOOKING FOR AN OPPORTUNITY TO SELL YOUR QUALIFICATIONS.

At this point, I feel like I have said so much that I need to recap to put everything in a neat shell.

What is cold calling? Cold calling is a selling technique. It probably originated as a salesman's way of penetrating new market or new customers. Realistically, salesmen cold call only to get the name of the right person whom they can then contact to make a sales presentation or proposal, not to make an on-the-spot sale. Initially, after getting the contact name, the salesman writes a sales letter to introduce the product and offer himself to come and make the presentation.

In today's lingo, the salesman who does that can be called a telemarketer. The telemarketer makes an outbound call to a prospective client whose name may be in a database provided to him. The telemarketer may or may not aim to make a sale.

A telemarketer's function may also be limited to simply making the initial call and getting indication that the prospective customer wants to know more about the product, and then pass this information on to the company foot salesman. This salesman may make the second call, ask for an appointment to see the person and make the sales presentation. Another telemarketer may have a specific function to sell.

Cold calling has evolved into a technique for discovering hidden jobs and selling oneself to get the job. It is also referred to as uninvited job hunting technique. Cold calling implies that the caller does not know anybody from the company he is calling and is simply taking his best chances. There is also warm calling where the call is expected.

To avoid the frustration of a rejected salesman, the point is to focus your effort with a minimum objective in mind the first time you make the call. The minimum objective may be to get the name and contact details of the person whom you can write a customized letter of application. That person is not the HR manager but the hiring manager, or the person in charge of the department you wish to join or apply for.

Do not underestimate the role of the gatekeeper (that is, the secretary-receptionist at the other end of the line). Treat him or her with respect, rather than as a mere telephone operator. Consider him as someone who could help you get through. Thus, it is appropriate to open with the statement, "Hi, I need your help."

Whether you are still with the receptionist or unexpectedly connected to your target, you must be prepared to carry on the conversation by knowing something about the company and its current needs, and how your skills can be useful in addressing those needs. When you get unexpectedly connected to the hiring manager, the minimum objective is to get an appointment to get a job interview or an informational interview at the very least.

Preparedness also implies that you have decided on a list of companies you want to focus your calls to. These are companies you are interested in working for and whose background you can look up and study. Simple math implies that the more companies you list down, the more cold calls you can successfully get through. There is a very conservative theoretical formula of $10=5=2=1$. Out of ten companies in your list, you may be able to get through to five of them. Out of the five, you may be able to get at least two accurate contact names. Out of these two, you may be able to get one appointment for an interview—a job interview or a mere informational interview.

Note that cold calling is a selling technique that even the most experienced salesmen can be scared of or get frustrated by. As such, it takes a person with the right attributes to make a successful cold call. That person must be focused, organized, patient, persistent, smart and humble.

Among these attributes, the most important are persistence and humility. Only the persistent person can always get ahead and only the humble person can cope with rejection over and over again. If you put these two attributes together, you will be on your way to successfully using cold calling as a technique in finding job in the hidden market and selling yourself to get this job in the end.

1. *Cold calling is an age-old salesman's technique. It is now an instrument in discovering jobs in the hidden market.*
2. *Do not underestimate the role of the gatekeepers, the secretaries or receptionists, in putting your call through. Treat them respectfully and as your equals.*
3. *Persistence and humility are the most important of the attributes you will need to possess to be able to use cold calling successfully.*

CHAPTER 14   INFORMATIONAL INTERVIEWING

14.1   What Is Informational Interviewing?

> INFORMATIONAL INTERVIEWING MAY GIVE YOU YOUR
> FIRST LESSONS ON THE ABCs OF THE NEW WORK
> ENVIRONMENT AND CULTURE YOU ARE FACING.

There are two root words in this term: information and interview. The simple explanation is that you get information by asking another person.

As a technical term, "informational interviewing" is attributed to the renowned bestselling author of the classic career guidebook, *What Color is Your Parachute* by Richard Nelson Bolles. He invented the term, so to speak.

The point of the information being gathered is still whether or not the interviewee qualifies for a job. But the information is gathered in such a way that the interviewer dances around the topic by asking questions from the point of view of someone considered an authority on the job as a resource.

But knowing about a job or a certain job description is not the only important objective going into an informational interview.

Informational interviewing is also a networking technique. Whether or not you have been referred by anybody, there is nothing stopping you in your being able to browse those company websites' directories and look for somebody to talk to or to be referred to someone who can talk to you. As such, it adds to your list of contacts in every industry you might be interested in, especially if an interview goes well.

For college students or new graduates, it is very important for them to get into informational interviewing before setting out for the working world. This process opens up to them the realities, prospects, and possibilities of certain jobs and industries.

I would say new immigrants are like these new graduates in a sense. Having landed in a country that may be entirely strange, the informational interview is a procedure that will enable new immigrants to be oriented and informed of the new work environment and culture.

Personally, I must admit that having been highly educated and having lived a relatively successful professional life back from I came from, I had the proud notion that I had very little need to adjust to on this side of the world. I thought I knew so much. Yes, why not? But not enough.

Who would not hate being required to have local experience when you have just landed? How and where can you buy that local experience to shorten this agony? I wish I knew where I could. But as soon as my feet started to settle to the ground, and I got myself little volunteer and paid jobs, I came to realize that it makes all sense in the world to have that local experience. As to why, I have devoted an entire discussion on it somewhere in this book.

The point being driven home is that an informational interview should be able to orient you on some local employment terms and practices even if you have not yet obtained the local experience needed because no one has given you the chance. The interview can very well give you your first lessons or the ABCs of working for a local company or within a new work environment.

The informational interview then becomes your eye-opener. It can be your acid test as to whether or not you are really ready to work in this environment. It is such a fallacy to think that work-readiness is limited to one's academic excellence or set of transferrable skills. In reality, it takes a lot of emotional and social intelligence to be able to make your way through successfully.

1. *Many times you do not understand why you are asked for your local experience. Informational interviewing will give you an explanation.*
2. *Getting ready for the new work environment and culture is not simple work-readiness from the academic and professional points of view. It takes a lot of emotional and social preparedness.*
3. *When you obviously cannot buy that local experience, you might as well be ready to face job interviews. Informational interviews are your practice sessions before the real ones.*

14.2   How Do You Benefit from It?

INFORMATIONAL INTERVIEWING IS THE WAKE-UP CALL YOU NEED THAT WILL TELL YOU THAT THERE IS MUCH YOU DO NOT KNOW ABOUT A JOB, HOW TO GET IT AND HOW TO BE SUCCESSFUL IN IT IN A NEW ENVIRONMENT.

In one of the first jobs that I got after having decided to get serious about my job hunting, I unintentionally put the instructions of one of my trainers in question, or so it seemed to her. She took it poorly that I seemed not to have believed what she said and had to double-check with somebody else. She rattled off her disbelief. But had I been given the chance to explain myself as a free man, I would have told her that I was double-checking was myself, and not her, and not even her instructions but the original instructions given to me by somebody else.

I had to double-check because I had dialled the numbers and talked to more than a hundred people only to be told that it was stupid to be calling those people after all, perhaps only to recoup my self-esteem a bit and verify that I had not misread or misheard the original instructions. But I was too shocked to even speak out that I deserved that piece of dignity.

But there was no point in emoting through that incident because my angry trainer turned out to be a really nice lady. She explained that she could sound loud and could be too straight-forward sometimes, but that is all there was to it. Wouldn't you rather have ten of her than have one who seems so nice and friendly but stabs you in the back?

An informational interview could have warned me of the different personalities and cultures of people in the workplace that I needed to understand and accept hands down. Although we expect that, because we know of a place like Canada to be the land of immigrants and to thus be a multicultural society, we do not appreciate the shock of interacting with people of other cultures until we work with them, eat with them, ride with them, or go to church or school meetings with them.

While the informational interview is not a shortcut to acquiring a high emotional or social IQ, it should at least prepare you for what to expect and how to respond to some situations. Your resource person must have been through a lot of tricky situations before he saw himself successfully climbing up the ladder of success.

From a professional point of view, an informational talk with an authority will also widen your understanding of the different directions that your own job hunt may take, or perhaps make you aware that there is an entirely new career direction that is waiting for you that you may have never thought of or considered. As to what are the requirements and skills upgrading needed to pursue this or that direction may also be an interesting area that can be talked about or explored in this discussion.

Trends, business profiles, and expansion or reduction of operations of major players in the industry which you are eyeing can be interesting topics that can crop up in an informational interview. This is important because it will give you indications as to which companies are worth running after or spending job hunt time on or cold calling for work opportunities.

You can also consider an informational interview as a practice interview for a job. Many of us might not have done job interviews in a long time, and this could be the chance to come face-to-face with a ranking individual and exchange notes and ideas. Yet, you are relaxed and will not suffer the tension of wanting to super-impress.

Above all, an informational interview may actually be that slap that will wake you up and make you put both feet firmly on the ground that you are dreaming too much or aiming too high at this point of your life as a new immigrant. After the interview, you may benefit from knowing what to expect at the very least and how to respond to a really challenging search for that elusive job.

1. *Informational interviewing is both a data gathering activity and a professional networking technique.*
2. *On another level, it is a way to acquire knowledge on how hard other people had worked their way up and to realize that, by working hard, you can also make it there.*
3. *Trends, practices and work cultures: All of these can be gathered from this interview, giving you a holistic point of view of the new work environment you are facing.*

14.3   How Do You Do It Right?

> REMEMBER THAT THIS IS A SITUATION YOU CAN BE IN CONTROL OF. START BY PLANNING IT WELL AND GOING IN REALLY PREPARED.

Simple. Again, plan your course of action.

First you have to yourself believe that you can do it: Face up to a person of authority and start acting like you are a press reporter gathering facts to create a good story.

Remember that as a "reporter," you are also the discussion director. You take the lead in navigating the discussion towards a direction that will be most useful and relevant to you and your "hidden" agenda. After all that we say about informational interviews, there will always be that little hope deep, deep within to stumble upon an opportunity for that job you have been looking for.

May I emphasize though that to have a hidden agenda is not bad, except that it is a no-no to bring it up in the course of the interview. At least it should never come from you while you are sitting there pretending to be a reporter. If it is the interviewee that says the magic offer, then why not. It is statistically correct to say that many informational interviews have ended up as job interviews. Interviewers sometimes leave with very clear prospects, maybe even an outright offer or a scoop as to when the next interesting job posting could go up.

Whether or not that is the case, it is very important to list the names of the companies you wish to request for informational interviews. The more, the merrier. I mean the more names on the list, the better chances you have of getting through. Read, read, read. Read about industry trends and updates, as you wouldn't want to spend time talking to a company CEO who tells you in the middle of the interview that the company is closing down in the next month or so.

From the list, prioritize the companies which you feel strongly about. Once you have set your priority companies, research them. An informational interview takes a more fluid direction if it becomes an exchange of notes and ideas between the two people who are talking. Remember the "hidden" agenda? You should also be able to project yourself very well in terms of your preparedness and interest to the company. It must be an intelligent discussion and repartee. Otherwise, you will be better off sending a written Q&A for the resource person to fill up and mail to your address.

As you research, questions will begin to form in your mind. Thus, you will be able to formulate your questions logically and reasonably. Prepare relevant questions. How you will proceed with the questions must be well planned out, so that one question leads to another and prepares your interviewee for the next one.

As a reporter/interviewer, have a pen and paper ready. Maybe you'll even want to record the conversation. Any recording of conversations should be done with prior notice and expressed approval of the interviewee, especially if it is done electronically or digitally. It is good to write down important points raised, names dropped, dates or occasions mentioned, because you will never know when you will need them.

One interviewer jotted down a date his resource person mentioned as a date that coincided with her wedding anniversary. The interviewer sent a greeting card to this interviewee on that date, and that made the latter remember the interviewer and invite him to apply for a position posted much later on the company website.

Anything can happen or can come out of an informational interview, including surprisingly landing a good job in the end. Although as I have repeatedly said, never, never mention about applying for a job while doing the interview. It is not proper to do so because you have cited your objective to be a mere exchange of information to which the resource person agreed. In fact, it is considered most appropriate to schedule such an interview when the company is not posting a job in line with your skills. But who really knows what can happen? The point is, go to an informational interview as if you were going to a job interview.

Dress for success. In whatever circumstance you find yourself, always be able to project a neat, well-groomed personality. While the attire is usually business-like, you should also be guided by the fact that you should be able to use good judgment in choosing the appropriate wearing apparel for each type of interview. You do not meet a neighbourhood house labour or settlement officer in a black-tied suit. On the other hand, you do not meet an executive banker in a tee and jeans. When in doubt, smart, casual attire will not go wrong. But always bring a jacket or blazer which you can slip into or out of as you see fit.

1. *Prioritize going to a company that you feel strongly about in terms of future employment. Read about this company as part of your preparation.*
2. *Go and dress up like you are going to a job interview. But it is a no-no to even think of bringing up that you are currently looking for a job.*
3. *Imagine going to a news beat as a reporter expecting to gather enough information to complete a story. Take down notes, names, and dates carefully.*

14.4   What Questions Can You Ask?

> SINCE YOU ARE THE INTERVIEWER, YOU ARE IN CONTROL OF THE INFORMATION YOU WANT TO GATHER. NAVIGATE THROUGH THE DISCUSSION TO GET ANSWERS TO QUESTIONS WHICH ARE MOST USEFUL TO YOU.

So you have established contact with the company in your priority list, check. You have the date and time of appointment with a resource person, check. You have reviewed the background of the company, check. You have your pen and paper, check. You have chosen the proper attire to wear, check.

Do you have the right questions to ask?

When you are making an appointment, it is most proper to indicate the estimated length of time your interview will be conducted. There is no hard and fast rule, but because you are dealing with a busy personality, thirty minutes should be a comfortable length of time and will most likely be acceptable to the prospective interviewee.

To someone like me who's such an enthusiastic and curious person, thirty minutes is way too short. But since you are asking a favour, this should test your flexibility and time management skills. Time management starts with asking the right questions and prioritizing the most important ones so that responses that will be most useful to you are more immediate. If the interviewee finds you very intelligent and witty, he will enjoy talking to you way past the deadline you two have set.

Since you are interviewing somebody whose function is within your line of interest or skill, you could start with **profiling the job**—what he does, what the expectations of his job are, where he is in the organizational chart, how his work relates to the other units in the company, how many people are working with him and what their responsibilities are, what typical career path in this function is, what skills are necessary.

Then you may move on to **profiling your interviewee** in relation to the job that he does in the company. How long has he been in his present position, since he started in the company, how he copes with the demands of the job, has he done any skills upgrade, what his own vision is for the company, what his working and management style is, what his own expectations from his employees are, whether he see his turf as growing or expanding, what strategies he has in mind to attain that.

Go now to being able to relate the person and his function to the **overall profile of the company**. What are the main business thrusts or objectives of the company, how does it intend to pursue its current objectives, what is the exact role of his office to these objectives, does the company plan to expand operations to achieve those, what kind of an employer is this company, are the employees happy here, what are its expectations of its workforce.

In an informational interview, you may also make it known to the interviewee your desire to improve your knowledge of a company or an institution which you intend to join in the future. As such, you may discuss a bit of your own set of skills and attributes, for the interviewee to give you an indication as to whether you need more upgrading or preparation to meet the expectations of job in a similar company. If the discussion reaches this point, be able to project a willingness to learn and openness to receive suggestions.

Bringing a copy of your resume is always useful every time you go out, especially for meetings like this one. But remember that you are bringing your resume not to apply for a job. Bring it so somebody, whose opinion matters, can critique it for you. In the course of reviewing your resume, your interviewee will get a good picture of your qualifications. As you continue in your discussions, he will complete his basic knowledge of you and your background, your skills, how your mind operates and what your values are. If you impress him, then chances are, he will have you in mind the next time an opportunity comes along.

1. ***Thirty minutes is perhaps the most that your busy resource person can give you. Manage that time very wisely in terms of being able to cover the questions that are very important to you.***

2. *Go from profiling the job of your interviewee, then profile your resource person in relation to this job, and complete the picture by relating the job of this person to the overall profile of the company and its business objectives.*
3. *An interview like this gives you a decent chance to project yourself. Carry out the conversation well, ask your questions logically, and speak intelligently. With that, you will certainly leave a good impression.*

14.5   What Matters After All?

> INFORMATIONAL INTERVIEWING BENEFITS BOTH THE INTERVIEWEE AND THE INTERVIEWER IN WAYS BEYOND THE IDEA OF WORK OR JOB HUNTING.

To my mind, this is an exercise that benefits both participating parties. From the point of view of the interviewee, even if the person on the swivel chair appears to be luckier than you are because he is now on a more enviable position of power and strength, he certainly stands to benefit from your conversation.

It should always be a welcome experience for the interviewee to hear out young and new professionals and gather their insights. In so doing, he is able to refresh his own thoughts and ideas. The resource person gains a different outlook perhaps. Or, maybe he comes to appreciate the fact that he is already up there and has successfully pulled through the challenges of the career climb and his life, in general.

As he meets or talks to people, the world around takes on a more meaningful perspective because the exercise opens his mind and broadens his point of view. He begins to see real people's concerns, enthusiasm, and maybe even fears. But most of all, he comes face to face with a real person who dreams.

No matter how we define informational interviewing, both the interviewer and the interviewee know that this is an activity that touches on an innermost desire of one person to find his place in the working world. He dreams, to feed a family, to pursue a career, to gather back his strength, to recoup his self-esteem.

From the point of view of the interviewer, the interview adds another person to his list of contacts and new friends, meaning that he is beginning to be part of this new place. Talking, laughing, agreeing and disagreeing on basic human issues at work during the interview process is so reassuring that this new place will not seem so strange after all. People talk. They laugh. They can agree or disagree. Do you ever realize what that does to a person who, like every other person, wants to be welcomed here and find acceptance?

For a new immigrant, the thing that matters is his own realization that he can do this. If he has been scared of job interviews or hasn't done one in a long time, then the ability to do an informational interview will mean that perhaps he can go through the next opportunity to sit down in a real interview for a job he aspires for. By that next time, perhaps he will be more confident and in complete control.

When you are an interviewer, it feels so different to be in control of the situation, to be able to steer the discussion to where you want it headed and concluded. To be a stranger and unemployed, yet still able to assume control of an intelligent exercise, is such a boost to one's sense of significance.

If success is not yet ready to embrace you, then significance can at least complete you.

To me, therefore, informational interviewing is an exercise that brings significance to two complete strangers. And the result that matters most is that, at the end of the exercise, they become strangers to each other no more, stronger in character and more confident to face whatever lies ahead.

1. *The interviewee, or the resource person, an informational interview grows from the exercise in that he also is able to gather new insights and fresh outlook, and perhaps renewed interest in his own job.*
2. *The interviewer, while finding himself unemployed, goes into a situation where he takes control and achieves a certain level of significance.*
3. *If success is not yet ready to embrace you, then this significance can at least complete you.*

CHAPTER 15   MENTORING PROGRAM

15.1   What Is Mentoring About?

> THE PROFESSIONAL WORLD TECHNICALLY OWNS THE TERM MENTORING, BUT THE HEART OF THE MATTER IS THAT MENTORING IS TEACHING UNSELFISHLY.

I was barely sixteen years old when I had my first student. I tutored a sixth grader, the adopted son of my godmother. While the English language basically allows you to use the words "mentor" and "tutor" almost interchangeably, the professional world owns the term mentoring. So at that ripe age, I could not call it mentoring then as I was far from being from a professional practitioner. But I knew I was not simply teaching my student the 3Rs – Reading, 'Riting and 'Rithmetic. I remember that each day that we were sitting together, I was also imparting him good manners and right conduct (GMRC, we called it then).

I was telling him stories of myself, some were a little sad but had happy endings, like how, at the age of two, I was given away to relatives as a result of indiscretion of two unhappy individuals, and that he was so lucky because he was legally adopted by a well-meaning and well-off couple. I would tell him that I was thankful that I was in school and this education would lead me to a good future, that any bad grades could be turned around if he studied hard and took his studies seriously, just like my "orphaned" and impoverished life.

I would correct his study habits, tell him how I did things and how well it was working out for me. I would tell him how teachers behaved and how that should be handled, how to handle bullying in school. I would ask him to keep his things neat, himself well-groomed and to always go to school on time, and to refrain from inexcusable absences, to always respect authority and turn in well-thought-out projects and assignments. I told him that a good education and the right attitude would be his keys to a successful future, just as they were to mine.

Now that my tutee is an accomplished doctor of medicine, I feel I must have been a good tutor and very well learned my first lessons in mentoring. I knew I always had it in my heart and soul to teach.

While mentoring takes on a more scientific connotation or technical meaning today, the meat is being able to impart to another person a set of knowledge, values, attributes and skills, from one's background and experience. Inevitably, you impart stories both from your professional life and personal life. I do not see how effective a mentor could be if he and his mentee are not able to reach a level of friendship and collaborative partnership to perform a successful job search for the mentee.

1. *Mentoring is being able to impart one's set of knowledge, values and skills from the backdrop of the mentor's own work experience.*
2. *The mentor must be able to share stories from his professional and personal struggles that enabled him to reach his current position of success.*
3. *The conclusion should be able to reach a level of friendship and collaborative partnership for a successful job search for the mentee.*

15.2   Why Would You Need a Mentor?

THE JOB SEARCHER NEEDS A MENTOR JUST AS A CHILD NEEDS A MOTHER.

Ironically, I never had somebody I could call my mentor. I had teachers, work supervisors, and loyal friends. And if the world says, your first mentor is your mother, I also did not have a mentoring mother. I saw my biological mother in and out of my life, but the world taught me how to learn from other people instead. It is sad, but there have never been hard feelings.

The job hopeful needs a mentor just as every child needs a mother.

What a tough thing to say about mentoring. Growing up without a mother is equally tough. How could it be possible for one child to grow victorious and strong without being guided by a mother? Why not? It could be. No biological mother ever took care of me. But the world is kind. The world is your classroom. The world has your teachers. So, it is possible. Perhaps a little more difficult, but possible.

But the truth is, the world is a lot better and your life so much complete if there are people who can guide you and cheer you on. People leaving their own countries and stepping into a strange place find themselves "orphaned" from extended relatives, valued friends and for some, even immediate families. Without them, it is so easy to feel alone, scared, and depressed. *Even the strongest person sometimes wants to lean on somebody.*

It is hard enough that you feel alone, how much worse if you know that there is a lot that you do not know around you, most especially the workplace where you intend to reintegrate yourself. This is a new world. There is so much to learn. People are different, and literally look different. They come from all cultures. They do not know who you are. But you need to understand who they are, how they think, how they work, and how they live.

Well, of course you can always try that yourself. Well, of course you can do that. But how well and how soon you can consider yourself out of the learning and groping stage, you may never know. If your personal provisions are not enough, then you do not have much time to waste to get to know all of those.

A mentor is supposed to shorten the process for you.

Mentoring is a process. It can be one-to-one straightforward process of interaction between the student and the teacher, or the mentee and the mentor. But I would like to think of it as cyclical. That is, the student learns from the teacher and the teacher learns from the student. Or, the mentee learns from the mentor and mentee becomes a mentor himself to teach other mentees. Only then can the whole significance of mentoring as a learning tool become real.

I thought that I was born extraordinarily good, strong, resilient. I came into my adoptive country with a successful professional life behind me, a stable past. But how many times did I cry in bed and want to pack up and just go back to my home country and have a more predictable future. Yet, all I needed was someone to guide me, introduce me to people, teach me about work culture, tell me about people in the workplace, and best of all, help me put my feet on the ground.

I needed a mentor.

1. *Whether it's defined in the technical sense or not, a mentor is somebody to lean on or turn to in your confusion, whether or not you are welcomed in the new workplace.*
2. *A mentor should be able to shorten the agony of waiting or erase the doubt that the mentee can no longer find a job in his own field.*
3. *A highly-skilled and well-educated new immigrant sometimes only needs a mentor to find a real story of struggle and success to be convinced to start his own story.*

15.3   Are You Teachable?

TEACHABILITY IS NOT ONLY THE WILLINGNESS TO LEARN. AT BEST, IT IS KNOWING EXACTLY WHAT YOU WANT TO LEARN.

The closest I got to being mentored was through the enthusiastic effort of someone from one of the help organizations that I went to. She became a dear friend, by the way. There was a process involved. As part of the registration process, she had me fill out a form and answer a questionnaire. In due time, I was introduced to a very gentle fellow who had recently retired from an active project management career.

Me, my friend, and the mentor met for almost two hours and really had a very lively and animated conversation. Unfortunately, the mentoring did not take off any further. This was not the fault of either my friend or my mentor. I think it was me. Oh no, not because I was not willing to be taught or to learn. It was because, at the time I got into the program, I was not sure what I wanted to be or to pursue. Project management was a good prospect, but I felt there must be something less stressful to go into and to learn. Thus, it turned out to be not perfectly matched at that point in time.

I don't want to think that somebody would not be teachable. People, one way or the other, can learn or want to learn. Even a genius needs to keep on learning. Even a champion needs to keep on competing. However, someone might not just know what she really wants. So the first important lesson, again, is focus. Before going into any mentoring program, you must definitely know what you want. You must be able to keep your eye on the ball.

A teachable person, with a correct idea of what he wants, can qualify for a perfect mentee.

From the point of view of a job mentor, the right mentee starts with no idea or perhaps very little idea as to whether he can make it on the right track. He may have his bagful of skills and scholarly degree, but landing on an entirely alien soil makes his stuffs not immediately useful and handy. But he has this desire to make it, and make it soon. He believes that he has more to learn than to teach at this particular point. And that bring us to my other problem as a mentee.

The other reason for the collapse of my mentoring match, and I am not trying to flatter myself, is the fact that I felt that I could be a mentor myself. But I needed to be successfully employed to qualify and more importantly, I needed to learn how to become the right mentee first. I hardly knew what I wanted—there was so much to want to be and so many areas or disciplines to want to go.

1. *You cannot be mentored if you are not teachable.*
2. *Teachability requires that you know exactly what you need and want to learn.*
3. *A mismatch between a mentor and mentee does not have to happen if the mentee is clear on his employment objectives.*

15.4   Can You Be a Mentor?

> ANYBODY CAN BECOME A MENTEE, BUT IT LOOKS LIKE A MENTOR IS BORN AND THEN CHOSEN.

I know I always had it in my heart and soul to be a teacher. Each encounter I have with another person is not complete if I am not able to share my knowledge, my thoughts, and my dreams. But in the reality of things here, there is a sequence of events that need to happen before you can become a volunteer-mentor. Even if you want to volunteer, a mentor waits to be asked to volunteer his services for free.

First and foremost, you must have at least one or two years of work experience in your field of specialization. The unwritten code is, of course, you must be considered to have succeeded in reintegrating yourself in that area. And I would think it is best that success is a factor because it feels better to become a mentor when you are proud of and happy about your achievements. After all, the mentee must believe the mentor because the mentor is his own success story.

The success factor is the inspiring factor. Remember that your mentee is somebody who comes to you with a whole set of skills and academic preparation. He comes with a solid experience of international background. Most likely, he is able to speak the universal English language both conversationally and technically.

As a mentor, the key is to help the mentee put all the skills he has in the right perspective at the right time and right place. He needs to be guided as to how to get off to a good start. He needs to know how his set of skills can fit into the local business environment. He needs to know how much he needs to adjust his work habits and work values to make himself acceptable and blend peacefully in the local workplace setting.

Newcomers, myself included, will never understand why there is such a thing as local experience requirement when obviously immigrants who have just landed do not have it. Only when they start being able to find themselves in real work settings or volunteer jobs will they begin to understand. Aside from encountering peoples of varied cultures and ethics, there are new things, new contacts and new ways to be familiar with.

When you are, for example, an experienced events organizer in your home country, certainly you have the right soft and hard skills to do the job. But how can you do your events management job well if you do not know who to contact for your logistical needs— venues, suppliers, events hosts, sponsors, transportation, support crew? Local experience will equip you with that knowledge.

I also believe a good mentor is a totally secure person. How would you deal with a mentor who feels threatened by his own mentee? He does not teach much because he is too busy staring at a person he believes wants to snatch his job away from him. He does not want to say much because he does not trust this mentee, as if anything he says might backfire on him or this mentee might learn so much that tomorrow he is ready to take my job. Huh?!

A good mentor must at least have his own wide network of contacts in his own. The best mentoring match is like a successful marriage. Such a marriage involves the mentor being able to find the right match for his mentee in the workplace, where the mentee can start using his own set of skills and newfound knowledge of the work cultures and business environment the two have talked about. This is ideal, but not a requirement.

The newcomer needs a foot in the door. He needs to believe that a door can open for him. The mentor is the inspiring factor. He has already made it. He got his foot in the door. He was able to successfully squeeze himself into the prohibitive entrance gate. The mentor has a story to tell, his own story or stories of people he has worked with. Mentoring consists of sharing those stories.

Lastly, a mentor must have a happy, giving heart. He must take delight in the triumph of other people and be proud of the achievements of his mentees. This is probably the reason why mentors are volunteers. They are not paid for their time and effort. They selflessly give them away for this cause.

There is a reason to pay forward, and there is time you need to pay back. If you believe this, then you can be a good mentor.

1. *Many successful persons have the ability to tell the stories of their triumphs and struggles, but only the good mentor can inspire his mentee to trust that he too can gather his own victories in a seemingly restrictive work environment.*
2. *A good mentor must be a secure person, and proud of and not threatened by the strengths and potentials of his mentee.*
3. *A good mentor thinks of this effort as paying back to the community that has welcomed him and raised him to his position.*

15.5   What Is a Mentoring Program?

MOST MENTORING PROGRAMS ARE PART OF THE SERVICES RENDERED BY THE JOB SEARCH HELP ORGANIZATIONS THAT ASSIST NEW IMMIGRANTS IN SHORTENING THEIR REINTEGRATION INTO A NEW SOCIETY.

I am not about to enumerate the different mentoring programs that are available locally or run by local organizations. It is not fair to the valuable service that these organizations render if I fail to give a complete list and honour each one of them.

There are as many mentoring programs just as there are as many of these help organizations. Well, almost. But mentoring programs are not limited to them. There are also similar programs initiated by different companies for their own employees, knowing full well that many of them have come from varied cultures or work backgrounds.

Most, if not all, mentoring programs are free. They are integrated into the profile of services of the help organizations which receive government funding for programs like mentoring programs. The mentors are volunteers. The mentors give their time without expecting remuneration except perhaps the satisfaction of being able to share their knowledge and skills.

The mentors are chosen. They are chosen to volunteer themselves. Some choose to apply to be volunteers, and the organization has its process of screening who qualifies to be a mentor. But it is disheartening if you apply to be mentor and are rejected. Thus, most prospective mentors would rather wait to be asked. Someone who is asked may say no because, as a professional, he knows that commitment is important. Thus, if he cannot commit his time, he may not agree.

An organization may maintain a roster of mentors, but can also specifically look for a new mentor if a mentee comes with an entirely different background or need from those already in their roster. If that is the case, the mentee may need to wait for his turn until an appropriate mentor is found for him.

The mentee and the mentor meet for a specific number of hours in a week, a month or some specified period of time. Some require 24 hours in a year or two hours a month. But the meeting does not have to be face-to-face encounter. Once properly introduced, the two can exchange phone calls or emails to communicate or interact. Commitment is expected from both parties to make the exercise come to a successful conclusion. At the outset, the mentee is made to write out a profile where he will indicate his set of skills, needs, expectations and short- or long-term employment objective. He should be able to communicate in English (otherwise, he might need to go to another program to first improve his English). This profile is evaluated to determine the type of mentor needed and whether the prospective mentee's needs and expectations are realistic or achievable.

As part of the overall objectives of the program, the mentor is expected to be able to help his mentee understand the new work cultures and practices, develop a network of contacts in his field of interest, identify the professional or skills upgrade needed by the mentee, encourage the mentee to take up courses to do that upgrade, help improve his communication skills in the workplace, help his mentee find a job or at least connect him to potential employers, and reorient the mentee on how to market his resume.

The mentoring program must be able to restore the confidence of the mentee in himself and in the new workplace: That there is an opportunity out there. That there is a space for him in this side of the professional world. The right preparation will help save him years to get back to his profession, and not a full ten years, the norm according to many.

1. *The functions or services of a job search organization become more attractive and perhaps, complete, if it includes a serious mentoring program.*
2. *Careful screening of qualified mentors and prospective mentees is important to ensure a successful conclusion of a mentoring match.*
3. *Aside from possibly shortening the length of time a mentee takes to go back to his trade or discipline, a mentoring program should be able to restore the mentee's confidence in his ability to go back and be welcomed in the new workplace.*

CHAPTER 16   GOING INTO INTERNSHIPS

16.1   **Do You Remember Your College Apprenticeship?**

> TO THE YOUNG GRADUATE OR STUDENT, AN INTERNSHIP IS AN ENCOUNTER WITH THE REAL WORLD WITH REAL PEOPLE, AS WELL AS A GLIMPSE INTO THE PROMISE OF HIS CHOSEN FIELD.

I do. I was a student of broadcasting. I was able to go live on radio or television as a trainee was as part of my course requirements. I went onboard an actual morning radio program. That was probably the first time I discovered myself as a spontaneous speaker. Imagine at age 19, I was giving tips and advice to homemakers and housewives. That was the show's format that I was trained for.

Barely two weeks after going on board, I was offered my own radio slot in the station that I apprenticed with. After one month, I received an offer from the government radio station to do my own morning show. Yes, it happened that fast and I was myself surprised. But because I was still a student, I resisted the temptation to go full-time.

Admittedly, it boosted my self-confidence a lot. Ironically though, I never got into serious broadcasting as a job, although I tried it for about six months during my senior year in university. That opportunity has kept me wondering to this day what I could have made of myself had I pursued that career direction. Certainly, I would be richer.

Most college students usually go into what they call an on-the-job training or practicum as part of the course requirements prior to their

175

graduation. Just as the one I went into as a student of broadcasting, this exercise is supposed to allow the student to use his theoretical knowledge to practice or discover how the principles he learned from school are applied in a real work setting.

The student is also made aware of how the work environment functions, including practices, the line of authority, the ranks, the logistics, and everything else that is related to the whole picture. Often, the student comes face-to-face with people that run the show, and the systems that are employed to conduct business on a day-to-day basis.

It is a practicum, or a practice session in the real world. The student may not only observe, but he may actually be able to participate in the activities of the office, albeit only those that are not confidential and do not breach security. He is given a taste of how business is conducted in an actual work setting.

It is not uncommon that student-interns receive actual job offers in the course of or after they finish their training. So while the student benefits in terms of actual learning gained from the internship, the best benefit could be the fact that he can so impress his trainers that his potentials become apparent and thus, may receive an offer to stay and work for the company immediately after graduation.

When we were students, we took on apprenticeship as an excursion or mere picnic. It was a chance to get out of the classroom and meet real people. It was time to watch your favourite subjects working before your eyes. If you were lucky, you became an actual participant, like going on-cam if you did television or on-air if you were on radio, and not merely assumed a behind-the scene role.

Student internship has its fun and it also its share of disappointments. We go out there imagining an ideal world to end up faced with the realities—disgruntled employees, asshole bosses, Jurassic systems, stinking closets, budget nightmares, killing deadlines.

But an internship is an encounter with reality, and reality is not a bed of roses. Not everything is nice, with sugar and spice. A good internship prepares us for the good and the bad, for a range of possibilities in the real world. It may not be the whole spectrum, but it's somehow a realistic glimpse.

1. *As a young student, it was much easier to think of going or not going into a much-awaited on-the-job training or apprenticeship because it was more fun than work.*
2. *An internship gives you a taste of the real world, but not the whole spectrum of the good and the bad side of the workplace.*
3. *It can happen many times that internship will provide a means for our skills and talents to be discovered, respected, and then applied.*

16.2   What Is an Internship Worth in the Working World?

> HOW DOES IT FEEL TO KNOW YOU NEED SOMETHING, BUT CANNOT GET IT? THAT IS AN INTERNSHIP FOR NOW.

The first time I read about internships in Canada was when the daughter of a dear friend emailed a news item saying there was a non-profit organization in Canada that matched skilled immigrants to employer-sponsors for an apprenticeship. This piece of news easily became a silver lining in my decision to migrate.

Shortly after landing, I lost no time in trying to connect to this organization. But at that time, I could not even come close to logging in to register because the system shut you out once they reached their monthly quota of registrants. For many months, I tried. It felt like I was being offered a piece of cake and just as I was about to reach for it, it was withdrawn from my hand. It was quite a disappointment, of course. But, if it was any indication, it showed how serious the problem is: How serious, not only the unemployment situation is, but also how desperate immigrant professionals are in trying to find their little corner in this arena.

177

In all fairness, the registration procedure has since changed. It now allows registration anytime, and the prior screening of registrants is based on the most sought-after profession or job position reported by its sponsor-employers.

Still, the whole exercise is highly competitive. And knowing how many unemployed professionals come in day in and day out, we may need a little more than luck to be awarded a much-coveted trainee position. And the trainee-position is coveted not only because people need a foot in the door, but also because it is a paid internship. It is like hitting two birds with one stone.

An organization such as the one just described has member-employers that pay a minimal amount of training allowance to the apprentices. I would think that, to most of these sponsors, they are doing this more for an altruistic reason, as a way to give back to the greater community, than for their need to train people and get employees.

Some classify these programs under corporate social responsibility. Companies find themselves allowing student trainees from the academe or as a probationary requirement for prospective employees in an effort to demonstrate their corporate social responsibility. A company that believes it is a beneficiary of the patronage and loyalty of the public to grow its business extends itself to this type of endeavour in order to thank its public.

1. *The poor economy and its effects on the business of companies must have sidelined programs of corporate social responsibility, under which external apprenticeship programs fall.*
2. *One economic reason that internships are so elusive in the workplace is the practice of giving a stipend or training allowance to the trainee.*
3. *Since on-the-job training is paid, the competition is great even for the very limited programs being run.*

16.3   Is Accepting Interns Corporate Social Responsibility?

> INTERNSHIP PROGRAM IS, IN A SENSE PURSUING CORPORATE SOCIAL RESPONSIBILITY FOR SOME COMPANIES.

In one of the meetings of the core members of an organization of working professionals in Vancouver, whose advocacy was to help skilled immigrants settle in, I suggested that we take the less trodden paths in helping new immigrants like finding mentors and arranging for internships. I thought that there were more sure-fire formulas with which the curse of the local experience could be morally exorcised.

While everybody thought that both mentoring and internship are significant strategies in empowering the new immigrants and liberating them from the curse, internships are not easy to obtain—not at a time when there is an overflow of labour supply, not at a time when companies are belt-tightening and cost-cutting, not at a time when companies are subtracting and not adding personnel.

I am not sure if many will agree with me that corporate social responsibility should be more manifest when the times call for it—not during good times and not during the halcyon days of the company itself. Thus, if sponsoring interns is considered a program of corporate social responsibility, why not implement or go into it at a time when the "market" needs it, at a time when the market will recognize or view it as an act of responsiveness and well-timed benevolence? Yet, how many companies are into it really?

Am I being too idealistic?

What is corporate social responsibility, by the way? Isn't it the ability of the institution to live up to its responsibility to the society? To respond to the needs of the society, and not to the needs yesterday or to the needs of an uncertain tomorrow, but to what the society needs today? It makes me wonder whether companies are able to read the headlines accurately.

Yes, I am being too idealistic.

1. *Corporate social responsibility is the ability to respond to the present needs of the society, not yesterday's needs, and not in the uncertain tomorrow.*
2. *Responding to the problem of skilled immigrants in allowing apprenticeships now is clear responsiveness and well-timed benevolence.*
3. *Internships are an effective strategy in addressing the problem of skilled immigrants on the issues that affect their ability to go back to the professions they once held.*

16.4 Are You Willing to Take an Unpaid Internship?

> THE WILLINGNESS OF SOME NEWLY-ARRIVED IMMIGRANTS TO TAKE UNPAID INTERNSHIPS MIRRORS THE DIFFICULTY OF FINDING THAT RELEVANT JOB OR BEING ABLE TO GO BACK TO THEIR PREVIOUS PROFESSIONS.

Internships or on-the-job training could also be implemented internally by a company for its own employees, for the benefit of new employees or for the purpose of preparing existing employees to take on new or expanded responsibilities. It is not a project, but rather more of a program that is run on a continuing basis as part of the company's human resource development thrust.

Although getting good, internal on-the-job training is as necessary as finding a hospitable employer, this does not exactly hold any promise to the unemployed, unwelcomed skilled immigrant. He cannot even get his foot in the door, remember? The core problem is his inability to get the relevant local experience that will re-launch his career in his field of expertise.

To get another view of the state of mind of some skilled immigrants on the issue of internship, I thought I should conduct a little survey, a backyard survey. A backyard survey is not scientific, but is similar to a research technique called focus group discussion: its results are indicative of the pulse of a respondent-group. Serious researchers often use input and trends gathered from a backyard survey to figure out the right questions to ask in a more scientific survey, and to ascertain which critical areas need validation or confirmation in a wider survey.

The questions I asked my respondents were questions I wished to answer for myself. I was looking to find out whether internships can be an answer to the problems of new immigrants. Given the fact that companies do not offer internships because they cannot afford the cost or do not see the need to expand their labour force, I wanted to know whether some people are willing to take on internships that are unpaid. And if so, I wanted to know how long they are willing to do the apprenticeship without the allowance.

Of the 25 people surveyed, 21, or 84%, said they would be willing to do unpaid internship knowing such an internship would be counted as Canadian experience. They viewed internships as opening the door for them, as shortening the time of their waiting to get back to their profession, or even just as a form of getting recognition and respect for the skills that allowed them to be approved for immigration. Of those surveyed, however, not one was able to get an internship or apprenticeship with a company, much less a company of their choice, since they landed. But they all had submitted themselves to volunteer work to gain their initiation into the workplace or some semblance of the workplace.

30% of respondents were willing do the internship for as long as three months, but 47% are willing to do it for only one month. One of the people surveyed commented that if a person was good, this would manifest itself in less than three months. However, assuming that you are lucky enough to be given an allowance, the threshold is at least $1,000 a month. Some of those asked reported that their only concern in expecting remuneration was, not as a payment for their services or skills, but rather as a means to survive or delay the erosion of their savings or money brought into the host country. The No. 1 objective is to showcase their skills and attributes.

But there is one intriguing and interesting comment one of those surveyed wrote that says "Even if I have to pay to be accepted as apprentice in one company for as long as there is a promise of job in my line of expertise at the end of the training, I will do it."

I do not know how to call it, but I am definitely aghast. I am totally terrified that this idea might catch fire and one day we will see it happening. When that happens, I do not know who loses dignity—the desperate immigrant or the apathetic other side.

1. *Companies do conduct on-the job training for new employees. But that does not answer the problem at all, because skilled immigrants cannot get these jobs in the first place.*
2. *My backyard survey says that skilled immigrants are willing to take an unpaid internship for three months.*
3. *Even if the internship does not open doors for them, they view it as recognizing and respecting them for the skills that they have brought with them.*

16.5   Is There an Alternative to Being a Company Intern?

THERE IS NO STOPPING ONE'S CREATIVITY IN TRAINING FOR A JOB ON-THE-JOB, EVEN IF THIS TRAINING IS NOT INITIATED BY THE COMPANY OR BY ANY ORGANIZATION.

I am not about to give up here for the sake of those now reading this book. Isn't necessity the mother of all inventions? There must be another way to do this.

I am making an intelligent guess that, even if all major companies in this country accepted a continuous flow of trainees every three months on a continuing basis, the problem or problems may remain unsolved for a long, long time. We are not simply talking about the unemployment problem or the difficulty of getting a job.

Let us agree that we are dealing with two sets of problems here: The problem of being able to go back to one's profession and the curse of the local experience imprimatur. And let us agree further that, in the meantime, internships present a strategy of allowing us to deal with both problems at the same time in a humane and dignified manner.

But the reality is that the scenario of all major companies continuously taking on trainees does not seem possible now. It may not be in the plan or budget at all. It may not even be practical at a time when the company is fully staffed, because no one wants to leave or to resign because it is difficult to find another job. It may not even be necessary because business is slow and revenues are not going up.

I asked somebody the most daring thing she would do just to get back into the workforce, and she replied, "I can challenge the company to allow me to work and assume my function or role without having to pay me for a minimum of one month and a maximum of three months. If they like my performance, then they can hire me. If not, I will walk away. I am only doing this because all things being equal, I know I will be hired."

I did not say this at the time, but at the back of my mind, I thought about how this situation almost happened to me. I felt very strongly about applying for a certain position at a company that I really, really liked. I almost dared the company to bringing me on board for free, with the condition that if they liked my performance, they would pay me retroactively. If not, they need not to pay a single cent and I would just walk away. Fair enough for both of us. But just like my respondent in the survey, I was only daring because I knew in the end I would get paid and hired. But I never did dare.

I have another friend who tried to hit two birds with one stone by enrolling in a course and asking to be taken in as a trainee-volunteer in the administration office of the same school that she enrolled in. Thus, she got Canadian education and Canadian experience within the same time frame. When she found herself down to her last $100 dollars, she obviously needed a job, but was in the same boat as many others. Luckily, somebody adopted her and put her back on track, and soon was

183

on her way to a more respectable status.

There are also schools that cap or conclude certain courses with a training package or practicum. These are offered by schools which are perceptively in touch with the reality of the workplace out there, along with the fact that there are academic disciplines that are best learned hands-on or trained for. In these courses, the practicum gives a lot of actual exposure and equips the student with the skills he needs to be able to adapt to the work situation after finishing the course. Thus, he gets both the Canadian education and Canadian experience that he so needs.

Internships may be quite unreachable, but if you are imaginative and resourceful, it is not like they are planted on the moon.

1. *Among skilled immigrants, the problem is not as simple as unemployment.*
2. *The two-pronged problem is the immigrant's inability to get a job in his line of discipline or profession and thus, his inability to get the relevant local experience.*
3. *Whether it is an actual company's apprenticeship or school practicum, only his limited imagination and willpower can stop him from trying.*

CHAPTER 17   UPGRADING TO START MOVING

17.1   Do You Have a Bachelor's Degree?

> AFTER A CREDENTIALS' EVALUATION, YOU MAY REALIZE THAT YOU DO NOT HAVE ANY BACHELOR'S DEGREE AFTER ALL.

Do you have a bachelor's degree? Check again. You don't have it.
So you came with a copy of your transcript from the university and your diploma? And you are really mighty proud of your good grades and your honour citations from school? Where will that take you?

For many of us, graduating from the university or college is an achievement of a lifetime. It is the conclusion of years of hard work and dedication to one's studies, taking an average of four years and even more so for those who need to review for and pass licensure examinations to cap the achievement of their diplomas.

Yet, what do you find out when your credentials are evaluated by an accredited international body? Your four-year course is almost always just equivalent to two years of college. If you had worked harder, took two more years to go for a master's degree, then lucky you. You are now a bachelor's degree holder!

I had my credentials evaluated and I am not sure how I feel about being downgraded to a post-secondary school or college graduate. Imagine how I went to night school for my Master's, heavy with a child at one point, to be able to get a little ahead of the pack and then being pushed back to just where you had once graduated from?

185

The other reason I went for a Master's degree was to be able to teach in college or become a college instructor. I kept moving away from this dream because I kept having children. The closest I got to teaching was doing employee orientations, product briefings, and hosting events. I planned that, when the kids get bigger and office work got more stabilized, I would go back to school and teach.

Teaching has been a childhood dream. I have always believed that it is much more dignified to grow old in the academe. In the school environment, the more grey your hair grows, the more respect you gain. That does not make me so vain, does it?

Now that I am literally reduced to having just a bachelor's degree, does that make the childhood dream an impossible one? What has this migration done to me? No career to speak of. Shattered dreams. Fast waning self-esteem. But let me think again.

1. *It may seem unfortunate that, back in your home country, you were required to finish both primary and secondary school in only ten years.*
2. *As such, you are two years short of your required school or academic preparation when you go abroad.*
3. *Minus those precious two years, you are virtually stripped of your bachelor's degree.*

17.2 Can You Get a Job Without Your Bachelor's Degree?

THE PROCESS OF APPROVAL FOR IMMIGRATION AS AN INDEPENDENT SKILLED IMMIGRANT LOOKS CAREFULLY INTO YOUR SKILLS AND EDUCATION AS QUALIFYING FACTORS.

Yes, you can.

Each and every local company will not ask you to show your international credentials evaluation certification or document. There are many companies that receive your resume as a tongue-in-cheek declaration of your academic background. If you say you are a bachelor's degree graduate of a 4-year course, then you are a bachelor's degree holder.

Perhaps the assumption is that the immigration process has filtered out the independent skilled immigrants who are coming in on the basis of their skills and education. As for the other immigration programs, like the Caregiver Live-in Program, there are separate, unique sets of requirements.

There are also opportunities that allow you to challenge examinations and academic areas of discipline. These will enable you to take fewer subjects in school and eventually move faster to your accreditation as, for example, a licensed engineer.

The licensing and accreditation issues are varied and there are long-standing concerns for specific courses. I am not about to pretend that I can tackle them here, even as just a quack doctor. If it is any consolation, the issues are continually being looked into and slowly, we will get there. A job is not a career. So you can get a job for as long as you are willing to do it, and have some skills to make your training on this job much easier and faster. Your willingness, your availability, and your flexibility are key elements. With or without a degree, you will need these attributes to land your first or your second job.

1. *International credentials evaluation is not a requirement to be able to land a job or find employment.*
2. *Companies that trust the immigration process believe you when you say that you are a university graduate, complete with your transcript and diploma.*
3. *With or without a degree, your willingness, your availability, and your flexibility are key factors in helping you land a job or keep one.*

17.3   So, Is It a Career You Want?

IF IT IS A CAREER YOU WANT, THEN THAT MIGHT HAVE TO WAIT A BIT UNTIL YOU ARE ABLE TO UPGRADE YOUR SKILLS OR GET THE NECESSARY CERTIFICATIONS.

When a friend of mine back home was waiting for his approval, he would constantly check on the status of my job hunting, perhaps using me as a barometer for his own dilemma.

I would repeatedly tell him, "There are many jobs if you are not picky." He could not use me as a barometer because, at a certain point, I was very particular about not landing at any kind of job just to earn money. I was hoping I could be choosy, and postponed serious job hunting a bit. There is a school of thought that says, "Just go and grab any job and everything will go from there."

The other school of thought is, "No, don't do it. Go find your own line or field of discipline. Do not waste time doing jobs that you hate."

Apparently, there should be a third school of thought, "Go, get any job. But do it part-time so you have time to continue looking for the job you like or for going back to school to upgrade your skills or get the certificate or license you need."

Just as there is a "fine" city, there is a "certificate" country. The first instils discipline and the second puts great importance on education as a way to get started right or move ahead. It simply means you need to get certified or licensed for a job, any job, not necessarily the one you want or you are looking for. A certificate to cut hair or do nails. A certificate to touch food and serve it right. Certificate this. Certificate that. A license to sell houses. A license to sell insurance. A license to sell investment instruments. So you can just imagine how overwhelming it is to get the license you need to be a practising doctor, lawyer or something along a professional line.

So if you want your career, you move toward it step-by-step. Whether it is by getting degree or simply passing an evaluation, to get an education or upgrade your skills is the way to go.

Schools or learning institutions are just about everywhere. They can be government-run or maintained by private institutions.

1. *The first school of thought is "Just get any job and you will go from there."*
2. *The second school of thought is, "Do not waste your time on a job you hate. Go find a job in your own line of discipline or education."*
3. *Apparently there should be a third school of thought, that is, "Go get any job. But do it part-time so you will have time to look for the one you really like or go back to school to upgrade."*

17.4   What Do I Study?

MIGRATION MAY GIVE YOU THE TIME AND THE CHANCE TO GO BACK TO SCHOOL AND STUDY FOR SOMETHING YOU HAVE ALWAYS WANTED TO GO INTO.

After having a successful hometown career, coming to Canada was like embarking on a new career. Being in a new place to start a new life gives you an opportunity to dream anew.

There were many things that I wanted to do as a young graduate, but because my hands were full with family and a demanding job, I was not able to do them. Of course, I loved my job immensely. I was able to make use of my talents, skills and was able to develop new ones as well. Even still, sometime in your lifetime, you will find there are things you want to do but have kept postponing because you are unable to find time for them.

Migrating can get you excited and make you realize that you might really have that time. And why not? If you have brought enough money to tide you over while you go about gallivanting and figuring out what you want to do differently, yes, you can. However, without enough financial provision, you will find yourself face-to-face with the reality that you still need to get a job at once. Lucky you if you find a job in the same area that you were doing back home.

Nevertheless, in that same job, you may find that you need to upgrade your education or skills. You may need to get your license or certification. I had to do that to be able to go back to banking and selling financial products. I was asked to study for my mutual funds license, which I did, although the job didn't come that soon.

Even still, you need to get your certificate or license to penetrate certain job markets. And it is more stringent and complicated if your line happens to be in a regulated profession. You also need your license or upgrades if you want to be moved or promoted at work, or maybe even ask for a raise.

You can also study for something you always wanted to do but never got around to doing. After getting my investment funds certificate, I studied "How to Write a Book." Earlier I said that writing is my first love, and they say your first love never dies. This is the reason why you are now reading this book.

I needed to do something or become someone I could be happy about, something that I could leave tangibly with my children and make them proud of me. I may never get rich but I can be happy.

The next possible step is for you to study something that you have never done but always knew you could do. Keep an open mind. What you see around tells you that there is a perfect way to go. Some courses are in demand and lead to higher-paying starting salaries. Taking that into account is simply smart and rational. Health care, senior care, homestaging, digital arts, special education, hair and cosmetics, and other areas of study will allow you to easily find work because they are in demand.

1. *Migration presents you with the possibility of studying for something you wanted, something entirely new, or something you may consider because it presents a higher chance of getting good employment.*
2. *Upgrading is needed to get some jobs, expect promotions at work, or deserve a raise.*

3. *Whatever you get into, make sure you are happy about what you are doing. That is the only reason that will make you hold on and finish the race.*

17.5   Where Should I Study?

> UPGRADING OR GOING BACK TO SCHOOL IS THE WAY TO GO IF YOU WANT YOUR CAREER BACK. SCHOOLS ARE EVERYWHERE BUT BE CAREFUL. MAKE SURE YOU GET QUALITY EDUCATION. SOMETIMES IT MAY MEAN - THE HIGHER THE PRICE, THE BETTER THE QUALITY – BUT NOT ALWAYS.

Schools proliferate. You almost want to think that going back to school and upgrading one's skills is part of the unwritten immigration package. Talk to anyone who has struggled and finally found success. There's a 90% chance—that they went back to school to upgrade and get a license or a certificate.

Anybody who wants a job can get a job. But somebody who wants a career needs to work harder to get it. You can get a job all right, but anybody who wants to build a career and go up the ladder of success needs to study and upgrade.

That has almost become a rule, a social norm.

With that, everywhere you look—on street signs, transit ads, newspaper stories, web announcements, mall walls—schools compete for your attention. They all seem to promise that they'll get you a job, but of course never guarantee it.

But also be aware that some schools could also be diploma or certification mills—schools that churn out graduates, without regard for whether you end up qualified or will get a job after. In truth, schools are not expected to offer or guarantee you a job. Yet, to my mind, they should at least be able to tell you which line or what is the trend in job availabilities.

When I was shopping for schools, I went to a community college to ask about their office administration and provincial instructor's program. I had noticed many office admin postings which I thought would help me get a job faster (the same with instructors' openings). I knew I could do both, but I needed the official certificate to do either, as usual, or to gain an advantage. The very simple picture that the academic advisor showed me was—for the same amount of time and money going to any of these two courses, I could choose between becoming an office assistant and earning $15 per hour, or a college instructor at $32 per hour. What do you think I should choose?

Schools do have studies and surveys of trends, like the one described. These are available for you to make enlightened and valid decision. First among these is regarding the type of course you need for upgrading or a new course in a field you might want to go into. Take time to talk to an academic advisor. Keep a vigilant mind and focus, however, because these advisors can also be very good salesmen that they might convince you into doing something you never intended to do or is not good for you after all. Remember that schools are in the business of enrolling students.

As to quality of education, I believe the principle is still the same in that, the higher the price, the more quality is promised in that product, assuming a transaction of integrity is being made. Courses may also differ in length of time they take to complete. There are short certificate courses. There are diploma courses. There are degree courses. Most of the time, you can work your way up gradually, because the subjects can be credited as you continue on.

Naturally, the longer the course, the more expensive. But getting an education will never be a problem in this country. The government has all the support systems in place to get everyone back to school whether in terms of student loans, grants, or bursaries. Schools also have their own scholarships in place. There are also free adult education learning sessions or classes.

What can be so amazing is the fact that age will never be a factor in being able to go back to school or to aspire to start anew. Nobody is too old to go back to school or learn a new craft. Nobody looks down on or frowns upon people trying to start a new course or a new life by studying again. As we said, continuously going back to school is like a rule, a social norm.

1. *There is no excuse for not going. The government has all the support systems in place to help you go back to school—loans, grants, bursaries, or even free adult education programs.*
2. *It is so amazing to realize that age does not stand as a factor in not being able to upgrade one's skills or go back to school. Nobody is too old to learn or to go back to school.*
3. *99% of the time, people who have been successful in re-entering their field or profession, went back to school or upgraded their skills.*

CHAPTER 18 DOWNGRADING TO SURVIVE

18.1 What Should It Take to Survive?

> YOU HAVE TO MAKE A DECISION TO SURVIVE. THAT IS ALL THAT MATTERS IN THE END.

"Your first two years as an immigrant will be difficult, very difficult," was said to me with almost 100% certainty, as if guaranteed. I had no idea.

Since I was "recruited" as a skilled immigrant, it never crossed my mind that I needed to acquire new "skills" in the first two years—how to sweep, how to mop the floor, how to lift boxes, how to climb ladders, how to stand in the rain and cold to wait for the bus to get to your eight-hour shift, how to pretend you do not know so much, how to keep your mouth shut, how not to react if a co-worker in the twelfth grade bosses you around, how not to eat lunch until your supervisor tells you to do so, how not to be insulted by flippant remarks like "hey you, come here" and "you know what I mean." Practically, how not to be your own self. "I am crushed," I once told a good friend. "I am completely broken."

But you cannot cry about this in the open. That was the most difficult part of it for me. You must wait until the lights are out or until you can shut yourself inside the bathroom. All that is in your mind is, "I have children. I need to be strong. They need to see me strong for them. I need to stand up, be strong and keep moving forward."

It takes a strong reason to want to survive. And you must be broken before you can be put together again.

To me, only my children were a strong enough reason to want to go on. Having made a crucial decision to give up everything I had and every success I had enjoyed in my country, only the reason of what was best for my children could be so compelling as to make me bear all the hardships and humiliations that I did.

To another person who is just starting out a life, surviving makes him think of his future, the future that he will be entitled to if he survives his present. He may not have a family or children of his own, but his own strength of character and focus on the brighter side of life will lead him to his future and to his success in the end.

1. *It takes a strong reason to want to survive.*
2. *Brokenness makes it possible for you to be put together again.*
3. *The only way you can get to your future is by surviving today.*

18.2   Is Survival a Decision?

> QUITTERS NEVER WIN. WINNERS NEVER QUIT.

We grew up believing that survival is an instinct. We almost intuitively try or want to survive because there is no other way to do go about this life.

But in migration, survival is a decision. I must admit that my decision to survive my difficult beginnings here was because I am a woman with too much pride. I will not want to renege to a decision already made. I will not want to say to myself that I have not made a good one in the first place. That is not to say that I think less of those who go back or decide not to continue on in this journey. I respect that very much. Each of our circumstances differs a lot. But to me, whatever the reason may be, it will be more dignified to have given survival a try.

Just being me calls for too much condescension to not go on or keep moving forward. I have never not tried to keep a promise. With this migration decision, I promised to give my children a viable option in life, to get a little ahead of the regular pack in my country. I wanted to offer them their passport to the world, so that when I am gone, they could continue their individual journeys and be allowed to travel along paths that are otherwise kept closed to ordinary mortals.

I have decided to survive because I want to set a good example. *Quitters never win, and winners never quit.* I am always afraid that my children will see me as cowardly or indecisive. I am afraid that they will become discouraged because I am myself discouraged and unable to fight my battles and overcome the obstacles. I am afraid that people will change their opinion of me. As I said, I have too much pride.
I have decided to survive.

1. ***For migrants, survival is not an instinct. It is a decision.***
2. ***Give a promise. Make it your compelling reason to survive.***
3. ***For whatever reason that you may not want to continue on, make sure you have tried to give survival a try.***

18.3   What Are Survival Jobs?

> SURVIVAL JOBS ARE THOSE JOBS THAT WILL WELCOME YOU WHEN NOBODY ELSE WILL. BUT MORE IMPORTANTLY, THESE ARE JOBS THAT WILL KEEP YOUR HOPES ALIVE.

As an immigrant, you will come to realize that, after all your inner struggles, the easiest decision to make is to try and survive.

How to survive is like a kit that has been prepared for you. Aside from the help organizations that have the kit in a neat package, you can go on foot and find stores and little companies that will accept your resume and welcome you as a "survival" worker.

Survival jobs, they call them. Jobs that help you get by from day to day, and help you pay for your apartment and utilities. Jobs that call you for work on a daily or weekly basis based on the availability hours that you submit to your employer. Jobs that pay you the minimum wage or a little above the minimum wage on a per hour basis. Jobs that you report to at a specified Start time but no definite End time. You may think you will work for seven or eight hours, and suddenly your supervisor will tell you, "I will send you home now or I will sign you out now" because work for the day is suddenly over.

Survival jobs are those you take two or three of at the same time and juggle them so you can fill up your whole week with at least enough hours of pay so you can get by. Survival jobs may be totally unrelated to the set of skills you had brought with you when you came in. They are jobs that may merely require your brawl or stamina, and a lot of patience.

They are jobs that you cry about before going to bed. Jobs that humiliate you, insult you. But as in all things, as the weeks, the months and years pass by, these are jobs that you feel nothing about at all. You wake up to them and sleep to them, then wake up again and sleep again. You do not even want to think about them.

These are jobs that will make your host country survive because nobody wants to take them, except the desperate or those who had not had the chance to think about where these will jobs will lead them. These are jobs that dirty your hands but feed your stomach.

These are jobs that will trap you if you will remain content with mere survival, if ambition has slipped by you quietly and you did not even notice.

Yet, to those who stay awake, these are the jobs that will welcome you when nobody else has, that will practically plunge you into the new culture, that will help you understand people, that will keep you intact, that will keep your hopes alive.

Survival jobs are jobs that will teach you to continue your battle, that will make you discover how much strength you have in you, that will enrage you from within to want to be something better.

In these same jobs, you might meet the people that will take you to your next level. Didn't we say that networking is still the best way to get a job or get back on track to your own field of discipline? If you refuse to meet new people by going out there and finding these little jobs, then you will not able to build the network that you need to discover how fast and how well you can get to where you really want to go.

Luck is not for everyone. That is why it is called luck, probably. Surely, there are immigrants who do not have to go through survival jobs at all. There are luckier ones who will even get real, non-survival jobs via the internet postings, which I have said are almost like a joke.

But it does not mean that, if you are not lucky, you are not blessed. *There is always a blessing in everything that falls into our hands.* You will know that in time.

1. ***Do not ever look down on a survival job.***
2. ***These are jobs that will keep you intact and make you want to continue your battles.***
3. ***These are the jobs that will let you discover how much strength you have within you.***

18.4   Will You Or Will You Not Take on This Job?

> THE BEST WAY TO NOT LOSE HOPE IS TO LOOK UP TO PEOPLE WHO HAVE BEEN THERE. THEY SUFFERED BUT HAVE SUCCESSFULLY PULLED THROUGH.

The account officer at my bank simply said, "Only pride stops us from grabbing a survival job."

And why not? You can always test how far that pride will take you. Then you will realize that it can take you only as far as your savings can take the beating. To some, it may not even be that. Some come with very little, and are simply pinning hopes on being welcomed by the new workplace, only to find out that the hospitality in a new country does not include that.

It is sad, really sad, to feel so unwelcomed in the workplace. Even in a survival job, people can be so competitive that you can only be so much or do enough.

After all, who do you work with in a survival job? Insensitive bosses who look at you as a desperate jobseeker? Pretentious supervisors who play favourites? Old hens who think they know everything? Bratty twelfth graders who grew up disrespectful? Emotionless workers who have been hardened by the unsympathetic environment? Cold-hearted fellow "survivalists" who may need this job more than you do?

It is tough, so tough, out here.

Do you know what will make you survive? Be with and talk to good, successful people. Hear their stories. Listen to how they came, how they stayed, and how they have kept their dreams alive.

The only way for you to understand where you are and appreciate the circumstances around you is to learn that you are not alone in this.

They have been there, probably even in worse conditions. Probably, they were in much more hopeless, more pathetic situations than what you're in now. Yet, they survived. They managed to rise above the circumstances to be where they are now.

Will you, therefore, take on that survival job? If you have no more savings to get you by, that does not give you much choice. But if you will, do not wait until you're at the end of the rope to get that survival job. Do not put yourself into a situation when you have to beg for a job or get a job that can turn your stomach upside down.

Do not get a survival job because you already incurred so much personal borrowings that all your little earnings will need toward paying these back. When that happens, you will hate doing a survival job even more.

1. **It may be true that only too much pride keeps you from getting a survival job.**

2. *As soon as you can, take on a survival job before you run out of money or have to borrow or beg for any job at all.*
3. *Even in a survival job environment, things are tough and you have to be strong enough to believe that one day you will get out of it.*

18.5   What Survival Job Will You Take?

GIVE YOURSELF ENOUGH TIME TO BE ABLE TO HAVE THE DIGNITY OF TAKING ON A SURVIVAL JOB OF YOUR CHOICE.

As I said, your decision to take on a survival job should not take you as far as desperation. You should be able to give yourself at least the dignity of being able to choose which survival job to take.

Survival jobs abound. The economy survives on the takers of survival jobs. How many survivalists made the Olympics events possible? Definitely the ratio is more than ten-to-one or even one hundred-to-one, for every full-time paid employee. I read unhappy blogs that say, at a certain point, immigrants feel this is part of the strategic master plan, pushing low-paying survival jobs on people to force them to spend money on an education to upgrade and get those required certificates. In both cases, the economy endures, and maybe flourishes.

If you give yourself enough leeway before getting into a survival situation, then you can still have some choice in where you will work. The most sensible thing to do is to find a survival job that will at least be related to your previous work or academic degree.

I would prefer to see my son who is a fine arts graduate in my country to work in an arts supplies store or an art school, whether as a sales assistant or a receptionist, rather than for a fast food outlet or janitorial company. For example, my marketing and events planning background made me accept work as a sales associate in a retail store as well as liaison work for the Olympics.

The simple reason behind this is that you get a little satisfaction for being in an environment that you are familiar with. You will be happy to be in a workplace where you think you can pitch in based on your past experience and have the hope that they will recognize your efficiency and skills and take you on a more regular schedule and in a more decent position.

Some take on two to three survival jobs at a time to be able to augment their family income. That is not bad at all. It is not bad to feel responsible. But may I ask you not forget about your dream, your ultimate desire to go back to what you were professionally or academically prepared for.

I would advise that the survival job should leave you enough time and energy to continue looking for other jobs or allow you to go back to school to upgrade. As most survival jobs are part-time and do not pay much, the temptation will always be there to take on more jobs. But hold on to your dream, please.

Once you have decided on a survival job, stay positive. Stop feeling miserable. Stop feeling sorry for yourself. Look forward and move on confidently. If the job requires a lot of stamina, be ready with your vitamin supplements. Get enough rest and sleep. Keep your Ben-gay handy if you need to soothe aching backs and muscles. Eat well. My son always reminded me not to scrimp on food. You need to stay healthy to survive that survival job.

It is, however, true that the survival job will not allow you to go to fancy restaurants or even to afford Starbucks for your morning coffee. But reward yourself once in a while so you will feel better. Always buy something you really like at least once a month. This item does not have to be luxurious, after all you cannot afford it, but should be something to remember each month of breaking your back at work. Share a little of that, too, with your family and friends. It need not be expensive, of course, but it will provide the joy of sharing your blessings, even in a smallest way.

There is no reason not to feel good, even in this period of difficulty.

1. *Unfortunately, your new host country's hospitality may not include immediately welcoming you into the workplace of your own choice or academic or professional discipline.*
2. *Hold on to your dream even as you take a survival job. Give yourself enough time to look somewhere else.*
3. *Stay positive. Look forward. Reward yourself and your family no matter how simple.*

CHAPTER 19   BE YOUR OWN EMPLOYER

19.1   When All Else Fails, What Can You Do?

> UNLESS YOU HAVE THE MIDAS TOUCH OR DISCOVER THE QUICKEST FORMULA, WE MIGHT HAVE TO BE EMPLOYEES FOR THE REST OF OUR LIVES. BUT THINGS ARE STILL POSSIBLE.

The entrepreneurs and successful business people will hate me for saying that. After all, the idea of going into business and being successful as a last resort or a desperation move does not sit too well for those who have put all their lives building their empires.

Why should it be that people who get rich are those who are in their own business? Unless you become a CEO or a COO of a large corporation and start enjoying fat bonuses and profit shares, you can never become rich when you are just an employee.

Yet, employees we will be for most, if not for the rest, of our useful lives. That is a hard fact that we all have to admit. Otherwise, if we have the Midas touch or maybe just the simple formula to be a good businessman, there would be more employers than there are employees, which of course does not sound logical at all.

It is not uncommon to hear of stories of some successful business owners simply stumbling into a business or going into business. A germ of an idea comes, and in a desperate attempt to find some work to do, the idea flourishes and opens up doors for success.

For now, I see two possibilities that can turn a person to own a business—one, he is born into it, or two, that necessity becomes the mother of all inventions.

To a hopeless jobseeker, when you cannot get a job, create one for yourself, or buy yourself a job.

As we go through this discussion, I will not kid myself into believing that most people will have so much money to start up their own fine-dining restaurant or buy a fast food franchise. What I am saying is, probably, when jobs are so elusive, trying something on your own may be a way to go.

1. *Going into your own business does not have to be a desperation move.*
2. *Some businessmen stumble upon some germ of an idea and turn into overnight successes.*
3. *While we may not all have the capacity to become successful businessmen, when jobs are so elusive, trying something your own may be a way to go.*

19.2   How Do You Start Your Own Business?

> AS IN MANY SERIOUS ENDEAVOURS, BUSINESS STARTS WITH MATCHING YOUR OWN INTEREST TO A CAREFUL STUDY OF THE MARKET.

There are three possible ways to do it: you create a new business, buy an old business, or get a franchise to an existing business.

To my mind, in any of these routes, there are also at least three things that you need: your personal interest in it, your money, and your desire to learn about it.

The best business to go into is one that you will enjoy doing and have the talents or skills for. It is better for a car enthusiast to start a car repair shop than for an artist to open a fruit stall, which is so totally out of her line and passion. They say, if you are not prepared to be on the job 24 hours a day, then you cannot be in your own business. If you will have to spend more than the usual eight-hour job clock to your own business, it better be something that will not bore you. It should allow you to exercise your own creativity and resourcefulness.

Unless you find an industrial partner, where you provide the labour and he provides the capital, then you will need your own money to start your business. Sufficient capital is important because businesses generally take time to break even or make money. Start small, they say, because a small business means small capital required. A small business is also easier to manage for someone just starting out or still experimenting.

As with anything new to you, you must take time to study the business and study it well indeed. Ask around. Survey people and places. Read business journals or trade magazines. Go to a school if there is one that trains people for it. Devour and assimilate all that you need to know or you could get your hands on about it.

Be also careful about joining the bandwagon or blindly following trendy business ideas. Trends are just trends, and chances are they'll fade away as enthusiasm declines and new ideas come in. Unless you are prepared to immediately substitute a new idea yourself and roll with the punches, then you'd better be safe than sorry.

If you are putting in your own hard-earned money, especially your lifetime savings or retirement proceeds, you should be very circumspect about everything. If this business will only be the source of your family income, then the risks are higher. It is best that one member of the family or other members of the family are gainfully employed somewhere else when the business is just starting. Prepare them to join you part-time or full-time later only when things are more stable and running smoothly.

1. ***There are three possible ways of starting a business: create a new business, buy an old one, or buy a license to operate an existing one.***

207

2. *There are also three ingredients necessary to starting one: your own interest, your capital, and your careful study of the business.*
3. *If the business is new, it is better that it does not become the only source of family income. Some other members of the family may find another job and contribute full efforts later when business is more stable.*

19.3   What if You Do Not Know Anything About Running Business?

> IF YOU CAN RUN A FAMILY, THEN YOU CAN RUN A
> BUSINESS.

I do not want to believe that anybody could not know anything about running a business. In many ways, running a household is very much similar to running a business.

You manage a cash flow in your family income, you take stock of your cupboard inventory, you make sure everybody contributes his time or effort in getting chores done, you institute cost-saving or energy-saving measures to cut expenses, you improve ways of doing things to get them done efficiently, you diversify your efforts to augment income by taking on part-time jobs, you control "salaries" or allowances so that everyone get their fair share, and so on. Those are values and practices you apply in running a business.

I guess it is more like: What if I do not know what I want to put up as a business?

That to me makes a lot more sense, because everything starts with deciding on what to take on as a business.

It will very different if one knows the ins and outs of the business. But to achieve that, you need to start somewhere. It does not happen overnight. At the outset, be able to study the business well. Study what your competition is doing, where they are located, and how they promote their business. If it is food business, eat out, smell around, keep an eye on what the others are doing. You will never know until you start learning.

Sometimes, an idea can cross your mind, and presto, you have a new business! It can happen out of a stroke of genius, out of a necessity, or by being plunged into certain situations. It can also be something that you have been exposed to as a young child by your own parents or relatives. Suddenly, you will find yourself in a new place that does not have this business, and you will have the opportunity to introduce an old idea in a new place.

A hobby can also lead you to it. Or maybe a friend who is already in business will want to expand or branch out, but does not have the money or the resources to do so. Or maybe there will be something you were doing as a mere employee for quite a long time that you now believe you can do on your own.

There is a lot of advantage to going into something that you enjoy, have been exposed to or have been doing; that friends or family can help you with, or an entirely new idea that everybody will be excited about doing with you.

In any of these cases, please note that going into business is best if it becomes a family matter, a family interest or a family decision. It is inevitable that family will be involved. In fact, it is best if the whole family can be involved. There is so much at stake in putting your savings to a business idea, and the stakes are higher if it will mean being able to put food on the table for everyone. In such case, each family member should know and contribute his own ideas, time and effort.

Many times, a person thinks of or wants to go into business, but feels he knows nothing and does not have the slightest idea of what business to go into. If that's the case, you can try franchising.

1. *It is easier to learn a business that is within your line of interest.*
2. *It is also more exciting to go into something that is new but will allow you to use your creativity and resourcefulness*
3. *It is best if the business becomes a family matter in which each member of the family supports and contributes his own effort.*

19.4   What Is Buying a Franchise?

> FRANCHISING IS THE SHORTEST ROUTE TO HAVING YOUR OWN COMPLETE BUSINESS.

Franchising is buying a ready-made business.

Technically, the term "franchise" means a license or a permit. To buy a business franchise is therefore to secure a license or permit to operate the same business. Franchising is a short-cut to having a business of your own. It comes complete with a brand, systems, signage, materials, ingredients, management and technical support.

At least at the outset, all you need is capital to buy the whole package and operate it. The very evident advantage of being able to buy a ready-made business is that there is less to worry about in terms of setting it up and operating it on a day-to-day basis from the technical point of view because everything has been bundled up for the licensee or franchisee, which is you. Should problems arise, there are experts to call or consult with for advice. They are supposed to be part of the package.

Franchise or not, you will still need the values and discipline needed to run a good business. You will still need to look after your cash flow, watch out for expenses, manage inventory, supervise people, manage quality of products, and the like.

You will still need family support, a lot of it. It is not good to be able to start a business of which the spouse is not supportive because then the burden of making it work and making it earn money immediately for the family becomes heavier. You would hate to hear "I told you so" remarks from the very people who should be in this struggle with you.

The key is being able to buy a franchise or type of business that is the right fit for you, one that you will like operating either by yourself or by somebody else you have picked. Both managing your own business or a franchise require the same amount of dedication and hands-on care.

When making decisions, always ask for experts' opinions or read about them in proper sources, and not the neighbour or the family friend who has never had any experience or business of his own. It is all right to hear out as many opinions as possible, but only the experts' opinion should count. There are franchise advisors who are the experts and the professionals in this, and they can be easily found as they are very active in their craft.

There are consulting companies that hold free seminars. They also give free sit-down one-on-one consultations to profile you and match you with the right kind of business and the right franchise that they have available. They usually do not charge you a direct fee because this pre-consultation work is already built in or part of the package fee of the franchise that you will buy.

However, you will still have to do make your own decision. And you can only make a good one if you had done your homework, that is, done your own research and investigation on the possible businesses that initially meet your requirements or criteria. When you are decided on what business to take, the consultants go as far as helping you find the legal experts and financial servicing companies to help you start up. Whether starting a new idea or buying into a franchise or an old business, capital will always be the ultimate factor. How much money do you have and how much more can you raise? There are banks and financial companies, but they can be restrictive, especially if the business or company you are buying has no financial history or track record.

Generally, small franchise businesses are in the $50-100k bracket. But that is the franchise fee alone. You will need more to set it up in a location, furnish the store, stock up the inventory, and pay workers. If it is a business you can initially run at home and among family members, then the start-up money needed may be a little less.

But in most types of businesses, location is almost always the No. 1 factor that can help you expand it faster. It has to be where your market can see it or avail of it conveniently. You can be good at everything when you set it up, but if you are not accessible to your customers, then you have a big problem there.

1. *Franchises are ready-made businesses. They come in complete packages.*
2. *There are consulting companies that can introduce you or discuss with you more intelligently how to go into franchising,*
3. *Franchise or not, you will need the values and skills necessary in running a good business, including the right decisions as consulted with the experts and not with merely families and friends.*

19.5   When All Has Been Said, Is It Really for You?

> GOING INTO SOMETHING ON YOUR OWN SHOULD ALWAYS BE AN OPTION.

I wish I didn't have to ask this question.

I believe I have never been a business-minded person. I am an expert in marketing products. You can ask me anytime to package a product to make it more attractive and sellable in the market, but to ask me to promote this product on a direct selling point of view, I do not know if I can do it, perhaps because I have not tried it.

However, when I was a sales associate, I had to entertain customers coming in to the store and help them buy things or decide to buy certain things. I told them about this product or introduced them to substitute products if we happened to run out of the ones they liked. I told them about the special prices or discounts we had for the day.

I had two occasions in which a senior couple hugged me after I helped them with something. They thanked me profusely for helping them get what they needed. The couples made repeat visits to the store. Even if they were just walking in the mall, they made sure to pass by me at the store entrance to say hi.

I had a young lady customer who was looking for a present for her mom and thought that she saw the item she wanted on display the previous day, but then it was gone. I patiently went to the back of the store and searched every nook and cranny to see if there were any in stock. I knew what she wanted because I had wanted it for myself too. Eureka, I found it! The young lady was so happy. She came back a week after with her mom to tell her that I was the saleslady who helped her find the nice present she gave her.

A few days after I was hired, my store manager told me I was doing a great job. I was very attentive to the customers. I was very helpful. I offered customers alternatives. I explained the features of the products well. And most of all, which is very important to my job, I made customers buy things from the store.

So does that make me a good salesman? Does that give me enough reason to try going into a business of my own?

I do not know at this point. Although at some point, going into my own little business is something that crossed my imagination, I still think I do not have the best ingredient in being able to start up a business— the guts. I am not brave enough. Perhaps I am not that adventurous or daring enough.

But I will always keep it as an option, just like self-publishing this book is an option. Self-publishing is like my baptism for doing my own business.

Sometimes, all that you need is to get started.

1. *It really is not an easy task to judge whether a person a someone will make a good businessman or not.*
2. *I would think it takes a lot of guts—bravery, I suppose—to try and make it on your own.*
3. *Nevertheless, I will not advise you to go into business simply at a point of desperation. After all, going into business is decent and gallant in itself, and people who succeed in it are the ones who become rich.*

CHAPTER 20

BELIEVING WHAT YOU DO NOT SEE

20.1 How Would You Like to Define Your Migration?

> MIGRATION IS A JOURNEY. IN EVERY JOURNEY, WE SAVOR THE MOMENTS BECAUSE WE MAY NOT PASS THAT SAME WAY AGAIN.

Is there a way to define what you are about to do or what you have done? The following are the synonyms for migration: Relocation, immigration, passage, exodus, movement, journey, voyage, resettlement.

In your heart, what did you have in mind when you decided to immigrate? Are you just passing through, moving on, leaving from, travelling to, or resettling in a new life?

Did you mean to really migrate? Or are you just keeping it as an option? Did you want to stay? Or did you just want to try to stay?

Can you see the future from here? What did you think you should do with the present? Eventually, do you want to go back to your past, leave your present here and continue your future there?

It will be very hard for me to choose to define migration for any specific person. Each of us is burdened by different circumstances and possibilities. The definition may not even stop at any point until we are ready to fade away from our past.

Migration to me is a leap of faith. While you have been made aware of what you can expect from the country you are moving to, that awareness does not take you anywhere. That awareness does not define for you what the future has in store for you and for all others who decided to leave and relocate to a new country.

I have been taught to look at faith as "believing in something that you do not see." Like migration is a decision, to believe is a decision. *To believe in what you have not seen is your test of faith.*

I have said "your destiny is where you are. What you will do is the result of what you do where you are."

If this new country be the place of your true destiny, faith will lead you to believe that for as long as you handhold with your destiny, what you have not seen will come to pass. They will mean the fulfillment of that promise of good life if you fulfill your destiny. If you believe that, even without seeing the light at the end of the tunnel in the beginning of your journey, then there is hope as you continue your journey.

The place of your true destiny should bring you a blessing, not a curse. Believe that.

1. *Migration has a particular definition for anyone who decides to go for it.*
2. *To me, migration is a leap of faith.*
3. *You do not see what lies ahead of you, but you believe that there is light at the end of the tunnel.*

20.2   What Do You Really Need in the Beginning?

> YOU CANNOT GO WRONG IF YOU BRING YOUR DREAM AND YOUR FAITH WHEN YOU MIGRATE.

There is so much we pack and unpack when we migrate, only to realize when we begin to settle in that none of the material things that we have brought with us will mean anything at all or will last us for long.

Having been through this, I almost like to believe that there are only two things that you could bring that will matter at all—*your dream and your faith*.

The "for the children" line is almost like a broken-record, so to speak. This line may be logical for those who have less in life or whose previous life has not been too prosperous, but what about those who had it good, a stable career, a solid fortune, a gorgeous and jet setting social life, a happy circle of friends and family? Is leaving all these worth it?

One of my friends back home called me suicidal. She said she had not realized that I was a masochist. She knew how much I gave up to be able to bring my children to this country. She knew how much it broke my heart to leave family and friends, and my wonderful job, to be able to give my children this option in life. They thought that I was so brave to get into this.

The truth is, I am the most cowardly person on earth to have made this decision. I was so scared that I would not have enough to leave to my children when I was gone. I was so afraid that nothing I left could ever secure their future. I was gripped with so much fear that they would not make it as I had made it. They were not scholars, they were not geniuses, they were not so sociable, they were not aggressive, they were not confident, they were not good enough.

In my aloneness, I realize that it was so unkind of me to think of my children that way. It was so unkind to ever think that God does not love them just as God has loved me. It was so arrogant to even think that only I could make it to a successful life. It is so irreverent to even think that I could be like a god and try to secure their own future. Can God forgive a mother?

God understands that I am a mother. God can forgive a mother.

Because mothers dream. Mothers have faith. My dream and my faith will see us through. Coming here was a fluid decision. As such, I feel that the long arm of God continues to lead the way in this journey of a dream and faith.

Whatever I have brought with me in the beginning may be gone, or almost gone by now. Yet, I know, only my dream for my children and my faith will remain in the end, and that, if I take care not to let these die, then I will be all right in this passage.

1. *None of the material things you pack with you will mean anything.*
2. *Only your dream and your faith will carry you along in this journey.*
3. *Keep them alive and you will be all right.*

20.3 Is God in Canada?

> FOR AS LONG AS THERE ARE RAINBOWS IN THE SKY, LIFE WILL BE GOOD AFTER THE RAIN.

I will use this chapter to forever remind myself that God is alive and is everywhere.

One day during the first six months after I came, I was feeling tired and exhausted thinking about my next steps. I asked for a sign to let me feel God's presence. I asked for Him to show me a rainbow. I love rainbows. They constantly remind us of the calm after the storm, of the pot of gold at the end of them, of a promise of sunshine after the rain. Lord, please show me a rainbow.

This is what I wrote to friends on that day—

"Today, on my way home, I asked God to show me a rainbow to assure me that He is there and that He is listening to me. All the time I was in the bus, I was looking up the sky but saw no rainbow. I got home, sat on my computer and Googled aimlessly until I got to You Tube and watched my friends' "Thank You'" video again, which I always do when I am lonely.

"As I was watching, I moved my eyes to the right of the screen, and saw listed as related video that of *Rainbow*, a song popularized in my country by the band South Border. I listened and I cried because God did not only show me a rainbow, He talked to me. And this is what He said from the song *Rainbow*—

"...Life's full of challenge, not all the time we get what we want
But don't despair, my dear
You'll make each trial and you'll make it through the storm
'Cause you are strong
My faith in you is clear, so I say once again
This world's wonderful, and let us celebrate
Life's so beautiful. So beautiful

Take a little time, baby
See the butterflies' colors
Listen to the birds that were sent to sing for you and me

Can you feel me
This is such a wonderful place to be
Even if there is pain now,
Everything will be all right
For as long as the world still turns, there will be night and day

Can you hear me
There's a rainbow always after the rain."

Is God in Canada? How irreverent for me to have even asked that question, don't you think? I am not about to let anybody think that God is not omnipotent. In whatever name or form you have known your Almighty to be, He will certainly follow you wherever you go.

1. *If you believe in your Almighty God, you will also believe that He follows you everywhere.*
2. *It is so irreverent to even think that He is not omnipotent.*
3. *Ask Him a sign if you may. The rainbow is my sign that He is alive and that He will bring calm after each storm.*

EDUCATION IS YOUR WEAPON AGAINST POVERTY. FAITH IS
YOUR SHIELD AGAINST WEAKNESS.

I grew up practically alone. I did not have a mother or a father. I fended for myself after being left in the care of poor relatives who struggled to keep me in school. Yet, I did not feel I was alone. My Tito (uncle) and my Tita (aunt) were such benevolent people. I would think they were people sent by God to take care of "orphans" like me.

Yes, my Tito and Tita were poor folks, but they gave me the most precious gifts anybody can give anyone—my education and my faith. They sent me to school and brought me to church regularly. They instilled in me the two institutions that are the very foundation of my whole being today. If one has both, he cannot go wrong one way or the other.

Education is your weapon against poverty. Faith is your shield against weakness.

Who was I? What was I? Without having been educated and having lived my life in constant faith, I would be nobody, practically nobody. And now as I write, I wish I can confidently let my children set sail on their own, but only if I am able to give them both or make them realize that education and faith in God are the only things they should hold on to in life.

But these gifts do not leave me with nothing to pray about each day. For each day, when you are in a strange country, where your education is not recognized as much, then you are left with faith alone. I know I felt I had been stripped. You will almost feel like there is no more dignity to speak of because you find yourself almost wanting to beg for the job you want. Only faith keeps you strong. You pray—

First, that your faith may continue to be alive deep within you;
Second, that you will be strong enough to take the beating;

Third, that you will have a reason to wake up each day and something to be thankful for each morning;

Fourth, that your family and friends will continue to be there for you;

Fifth, that one day, you will look back and be thankful that you have weathered the storm.

1. ***Pray that you continue to live in faith, with your family and friends.***
2. ***Pray for strength to take the beating, and a reason to wake up each morning***
3. ***Pray that one day you can look back and thank God that you have persevered.***

20.5   Quo Vadis, Fellow Migrant?

WHEN YOU ARE A NEW MIGRANT, THE BEST SHIELD AGAINST DISCOURAGEMENT IS TO TRY TO THINK ONLY OF THE PRESENT, WITH FAITH IN YOUR HEART.

What now? What for? What then? What else?

Moving forward is not easy advice to take, especially if you are not sure whether you can do it.

When I first decided to write a book, I said I would not do it if I could not be honest and strong enough to move forward. I did not want to end up discouraging people or making them think they had made a very costly mistake by leaving their home countries.

I always believe that things happen for a reason. If such a thing happens in veritable circumstances, then more the reason it was meant to be.

Have you ever heard of the old man's words of wisdom—*the past is gone, tomorrow is not yet, today is all you have?*

When you are new migrant, the best shield against discouragement is to try to think only of the present with faith in your heart.

If we keep thinking of what we gave up to come, what we left behind to get here, we cannot move happily forward. When we fear about the future so much because we are unable to get the recognition and acceptance that we thought would be accorded to us, we cannot confidently move forward. When we believe only what we see, then we cannot faithfully move forward.

Happy. Confident. Faithful. I want you to remember these attributes.

When I was crying over the small jobs that I had in the beginning, the message to me was that I needed to prove myself first in the little things before I could be trusted with big and mighty things. Plus, I realized that I was being irreverent by calling them small jobs, because without these jobs and the people that do these jobs, who would run the very cogs that keep a country moving forward?

Happy. Confident. Faithful. These are the values by which you should live your life from day to day.

Your faith—**believing that which you have not seen**—is your edge, your triumph. Not many may have it in them.

And please, remember the rainbow.

1. *I want us to keep moving forward because, under the veritable circumstances that we are here, there are equally veritable reasons that we need to stay.*
2. *Happiness, confidence, and faith. Remember these words as you slowly move forward.*
3. *Believing in what yet you do not see will be your edge and your source of triumph in the very end.*

10 Reasons Why You Cannot Get a Job

You Do Not Have a Job Because...

1. You blame it on the economy.

I am a bit cynical about blaming the economic crisis for not finding a job. There are hundreds of job hunting books out there, written all around the world and released at different times and seasons of long ago. Does that mean that, throughout history, economies everywhere have never been out of crisis?

It does seem more logical to believe that the relationship between the economy and unemployment lies in the perfect or near-perfect match between the skills of job hunters and the needs of the employment market at various points of the economic cycle.

Although the arithmetic is true, that in a crisis, there are fewer jobs, what we wish to address is how flexibly you can switch from one role to another in order to find a new work environment. Therefore, no matter the state of the economy, you will have this ability to assume different functions and thus stay on the job or get a new job.

Without flexibility, a person who works in a battered industry may find himself jobless for a while until he is able to learn something new or change career paths.

The bottom line is, for the multi-skilled individual or someone quick to adapt to market demands, including the willingness to relocate to an area where the unemployment rate is much lower, then there is no such reason as economic crisis for not having a job.

2. You do not know what you want.

I plead guilty. Upon immigrating and finding myself free from the pressure of a full-time job, I felt like I had just been released from prison. I came and saw that suddenly there was a chance to do many new things, learn new crafts, go back to school, do volunteer work, build new networks, see new places. I wanted to do practically all of them and did not even know how to start.

But in reality, I did not know what I really wanted. It came very fast and without realizing it, one year had passed and I had not accomplished any serious job hunting. While I did not know what I wanted, I was not wasting my time. I did so much and met a lot of good people in the process. It is not good to not know what you want. Unfortunately for some, it may not even be possible to consider this question, because they need to put food on the table, a roof over their heads, not to mention obtain the layers of clothes to bundle up in the cold.

However, my initial lack of focus enabled me to see the big picture. While focus is a positive attribute, it can also be crippling. Too much of it can cramp your ability to explore the horizon. Otherwise, you would not have this book in your hand today.

This is not to say that what I did was right or is applicable to everybody. The sooner you come to terms with what you want to be, the better. In so doing, you will be able to focus your own job hunt at something specific or upgrade your skills so that you will get a job faster.

3. You are not in the right place.

Well, of course, your host country is your home now. After having just gone through the agony of moving and settling in, the thought of packing those bags again might not sit too well with you so soon.
Certainly, the decision to come is not a simple matter, especially if there is a whole family involved. But I think the sooner you do it, the better, especially when there are no new roots at all for you and the children.
Relocating yourself to another province or city (in the same host country,

of course) is always an option. It is not an easy option, I know. But when you start realizing that there are just too many of you here scrambling in a certain place for too little, then the brave and mighty you might just have to consider moving to where unemployment rates are lower.

4. You want a career from the outset.

I have repeatedly differentiated a job from a career in this book. In fact, I have been using the phrase "job hunting" merely as a convenient terminology. Job hunting is easy, but a career search isn't. The truth of the matter is, there are steps in establishing your career.
The two most critical ones are upgrading your skills and finding a job, and not necessarily in that order. The key is to be able to find a job within the industry where you want to establish a career, and then find the time to go back to school and earn your license or certificate or simply to upgrade. This requires hard work indeed.
 Actually, you have a clear choice to not to work that hard. But that requires forgetting about establishing a career. No pain, no glory.

5. You do not have local experience.

To someone who has just landed, and is looking for a job, this can be the most ridiculous requisite, indictment, accusation, measure of inadequacy, that any local company can give you as a reason for rejecting your application. It is disdainful, absolutely preposterous, if not completely offensive.

But hold it.

It is not like you cannot get any work or work experience at all if you are newly-landed. I got a job. Many get their first jobs. Even volunteer work is considered an experience. Even a humble sales job at a tiny retail store is an experience. Even your school involvement is an experience.

After I had a bit of work, both paid and unpaid, around the city, and had met a lot of people of various cultures and persuasion, I saw exactly why they want you to have "local experience".

It is not necessarily to discriminate against you. It is not even to teach you skills, because you already have them for sure. It is because they want you to be successful. You think you know the work or have the skills to do the work. The local workplace culture can be so different and intimidating, you would want to quit. You want to quit not because you cannot do the job, but because you do not understand your co-workers. You cannot seem to adjust to people. The differences can go from good to bad, from best to worst.

Once, I was caught with mouth wide open when a twelfth grader (she was 17 and she could work) ordered me around. She wanted me to go over to her till and help her with what she was doing. And she said that aloud in front of all customers. I did not immediately wait upon to her, as I was finishing a job given by the real boss and told her she would have to wait. After both our shifts, she gave me a dagger look and would not talk to me. In retrospect, a friend told me that I should not worry because it was more correct to finish the manager's task before helping others out with their own jobs.

I was also shocked at how others were able to stretch a one hour-worth of work to take up half a day. I had made my own statistical calculation of the same task. When I was asked to do some outbound calls with no output count imposed, after two hours of doing the calls, I took it upon myself to calculate how many calls I could make in an hour, plus or minus. I went back to the supervisor and told her that how long it would take me to call 300 people in my list, assuming there were no interruptions and other tasks given. All that I was told was "Doesn't matter, just make the calls." Is that good or bad?

There are work cultures and work ethics to learn or un-learn. There are people to adjust to, people entirely strange from your own kind. Nevertheless, the universal work values will remain unchanged— respect for others, honesty and dedication, to name a few. But until you find yourself in the same ground with new peoples, you will never be able to discover how things can be so difficult and different.

6. You do not speak good English.

I would say, maybe, but not quite. In some specific jobs, yes.

I would think it is more of you shying away from work that involves communicating to people rather than the hiring officer discriminating against your inability to speak the English language very well.

First, I realize that there are a lot of jobs that do not require perfect English, meaning the grammar, the syntax, the pronunciation, or even the accent do not need to be perfect. It is more important that you can say what is on your mind, staccato English notwithstanding. Unless you are applying for a writing or teaching position, or something that really explicitly requires high proficiency in English, you will get away with your current level of proficiency.

However, you are, of course, at a great disadvantage if you do not speak the English language well, because it is the medium of instruction in schools and of business communication in many, if not all, prestigious companies.

7. You have not been properly guided.

When a friend from my home country asked me how I was doing with my job search, I said there was not much to say because it had not been good. He said the advice that he got was that all he needed to do was to sit before the computer the whole day, every day and submit applications on all the job sites he could log on to.

I will not pass conclusive judgment, but anybody reading this and who had been through job-hunting that way can certainly make an opinion. The Internet is your friendly home companion, but it is not necessarily your friendly headhunter.

Another friend advised a newly-landed to simply walk around downtown, visit shops, and go in just to check if they are hiring. Two weeks after she had landed, she got a job in one of the brand stores. As she was working at that store job part-time, she continued to check out the job bulletins of the help organization she signed up with. One month later, she landed a better hotel management job, something nearer the line of work she wanted to do.

You could also be in a situation in which no one is willing to give you any advice at all (although I do not know how that could be possible), because, one, they really do not care at all, two, you have not really asked, or three, they do not want to be blamed for anything that may go wrong with you.

8. You are too much.

Oh yes. You can be overqualified.

Well, they do not tell you that. But the hiring manager or the interviewer will look at you and at the back of his mind think, "This guy will not stay long. He will get bored with this job. He will just go and find what he wants soon enough."

As a mature individual or a professional, you should be able to understand that. From the point of view of the company, it is very expensive to keep hiring or training new people on the job. If they suspect that you will just leave anyway, they would rather not bring you onboard at all.

As I said earlier in this book, the HR person or the interviewer can also be very human. He will pass judgment and not be able to be totally objective all the time. If he sees you as a threat to his own job or to his own boss, then your chances of being hired will be slimmer.

In other words, give only what is asked for, say only what is asked about. It is very important that you carefully study the required qualifications to a job posting. If it says that a university degree is enough, then it does not need your master's degree. If certain knowledge of a computer language is required, list only those that match the requisites. Knowing too much or having too many qualifications may not necessarily work to your advantage.

9. You are too old.

Ok, nobody says that straight.

It is possible you yourself feel you are too old, or probably do not have the brawl anymore to endure a strenuous or demanding job. When I was shopping for jobs in a mall, I would, on my own accord, refuse to try and ask at stores that I found too trendy or too juvenile. And there are a lot of those! The vanity in me refuses to be called the granny of the group.

There are also jobs that can easily bore or annoy a mature, experienced person more than they do a fledgling. I am guilty of this. I like working with people who can pick up instructions quickly or who can work with very minimum supervision. I simply just get exasperated if I have to repeat myself too often. If you were a supervisor and now find yourself starting from the ranks again, there is also quite an adjustment to make having to follow instructions instead of giving them, or minding details again.

But in the jobs that I got, the age ranged from twelfth graders to retirees, and nothing mattered. The issue is whether you can do the job. But nobody is given special treatment either. If you are older, you do not take your break ahead of the younger ones. You take your break in the order that you came in or go only when you are told you can by the supervisor. That's fair and simple. Also, if you are older, the younger ones will not help you finish your job.

However, I do not let that get to me. I still help the older ones or the one with a cane if they want me to. Be sure to help only if they want you to. The older workers will not let the younger ones insult them that way. You get the same pay anyway.

10. You are too proud.

A successful immigrant-banker once said he believes it is only pride that keeps people from taking on odd jobs or starting all over again.

The thing is, the same proud people do not realize that they are in a new country, a place where no one really looks down on people doing menial jobs. A place where just about everybody started the same way, or almost. A place where each person hopes to get over the hump and find the silver lining one day, perhaps not soon, but believes he will find it for sure. Why? Because they know. They see these successful people all around them.

No one looks down on you for having a small job, or not finding a job quickly. It is all in your mind. You simply cannot accept it. You keep looking back. You have not amply psyched yourself into believing that life will no longer be the same. Get over that and you will find that job.

How I Got My First Serious Job

The manner by which I got my first serious job is probably not as dramatic as to how other immigrants got theirs. But I am sharing the story just the same to give a simple testament as to how most of the rules I have prescribed in the job hunting part of this book have worked or not worked for me.

Having no idea whatsoever as to how things were done in my new country, I began my job hunt through **networking** way back from my home country. A client of the bank where I used to work gave a positive email introduction to his friend in a big bank headquartered in Toronto. Several email exchanges later, I got so far as being interviewed by their HR over the phone, taking their online tests for my role, and getting interviewed by the manager of a branch of my choice in Vancouver.

When I passed all of these tests, I was advised that I needed to **upgrade my skills** by earning my certificate to sell mutual funds. The Investments Funds Course of Canada can take one year to complete. I thought that was too long. They said the good ones finish and pass it in three months. I took the course and passed it in one month. I immediately informed them that I had passed the course. After the congratulations, they said they would call to inform me when the position became available. Even one year after I passed the course, I never got the call for that particular job. It was supposed to be a first-level officer position.

The reason given was that, while the company was used to quick turnovers in the past, that particular year, nobody was leaving his job. They surmised it must be the crisis and people were holding on to their jobs because they knew it was so difficult to get a new one. I never believed though that any crisis will be the reason for not being able to get a job.

There is no economic crisis in the bigness of my God.

But during that one year, I didn't feel the pressure to go and try harder at finding a job. This is probably because I thought this was a chance for me to mother my kids, take up new things, make new friends, or simply rest after working the 9-5 life for years and years since after college.

In between mothering and discovering, I **volunteered**. I got involved in my community, and did what I knew best—planning events, coordinating people, facilitating meetings. I also did simple kitchen duties during fund raising parties and gatherings. I **networked** and met a lot people. We talked endlessly about how life was around here. They comforted, cajoled, encouraged, cautioned, strengthened. They told me their own humble stories to reassure me that most everyone goes through similar experiences and advised never to give up, but to just keep going and going.

I signed up with at least four different **help organizations** for new immigrants and job search programs. Except for one, I never officially concluded the programs I signed up for. I went to a **two-week resume writing class** and it was worth it.

But more than the content and the substance of these programs, the people I met in these help organizations were a source of hope and strength. Whether it was part of their job or not, it warmed my heart that I would be one of the first people they would inform if they learned about a job fair, a job workshop, or a job opening. They would push me to give it my shot, never waning in following up and egging me on all the time.

Within the same year, I must have composed more than one hundred versions of my resume that I **emailed or sent online or via snail mail**. I had paid money to **subscribe to an internet-based job site** in the education sector that never got back to me with any job hope at all. Of the hundred resumes I sent online, only one called me for an interview, and only one company had the courtesy to tell me they have finished reviewing my application and that no suitable position was available at that time. All the rest, I received a *"Thank You. Your Resume Has Been Successfully Submitted,"* message almost instantly and that was it.

So within a span of one year, I had **two job interviews**, one from the first networking opportunity, and the second from the internet job site. Also, within that span of one year, I realized that my money had gone down to more than half of what I brought in. Yet, we were living as simply as we could, and did not take even one family holiday. I also had two grown-up sons incurring their own student loans in order to upgrade their own skills.

One day after that one year, a college chum whom I met again in one of my volunteer works, invited me for a dinner reunion with one of our classmates who had also arrived not over two months earlier. But this classmate had a job two weeks after she had landed, and had moved to a better one a month thereafter. I was so surprised because here I was one year landed and still without a job. What did she do?

She walked around downtown and **walked in at some stores** she wanted to work for. Once she got one of these, she continued **to network with the help organization** she affiliated with and checked out their job placement list almost every day. That was how she got her second job. That dinner reunion was a Saturday evening. Both of my classmates encouraged me to give my job hunting some serious try. I promised that the following day I would walk around my favourite mall. I didn't want to walk around downtown because it was December and I thought it was too cold to be walking around the streets.

One of my sons wanted to buy something from the mall and so we ended up going that following Sunday. I told him that I would take a bit of a detour and see if I could find a job by just **walking in**. We tried two stores and then went for lunch. I was itching to go and try again, so I told

233

my son that I would leave him to his lunch for a while and see if I could apply at one or two more stores.

I went in to a Christmas store, or so I call it, and within fifteen minutes of waiting, I was called in by the manager. I was asked to please describe myself. I only got to as far as the third sentence of my WAP script, when I was hired on the spot. I even had to ask permission to go back and send my son home. I had this Christmas store job for one month, for it was fairly seasonal.

In the middle of that job, one of my ever faithful rah-rah girls from the help organization I was familiar with called and literally pushed me to **go to a job fair**. I didn't even know which company was hiring, but I went and was hired for a temporary admin job for the Vancouver 2010 Olympics. I did this job for two months.

In between this admin job, I was being interviewed and processed to relieve the assistant managers of a small neighbourhood coffee shop should any one of them go on a holiday. I got the on-call job, but it didn't come through, because after I winded up with that admin job, I was signed up to do a frontline job for a bank. Yes, this was through that same prospective bank-employer that I had networked with when I first landed.

I am therefore glad to be back to the industry where I had started my career in my own country. How I really got this frontline job is another story of great faith and perseverance. Suffice it to say for now that, within the span of the year that my resume sat in this bank's files, I sporadically continued to send "hello" emails to the HR contact person who had been introduced to me.

My advice is that, while doing a part-time or temporary job, it is important never to give up on finding your mainstream employment. Hold on to your dream. Do not allow yourself to get trapped in the middle of earning rent money and fatigue.

I stayed focused, reminding myself that the store job and admin job were not what I came to this country for. It was not what I wanted. They had helped me to keep my hopes alive so that I would be able to go back to my main line, not in a small, unknown company but in a big one. I remember one of our speakers in a job search workshop telling me, "You know, you sound like you want to hit the big time. You know, joining a big-time company, not those small companies..." Confidently, I responded yes. One day, I know I will.

Indeed, that big-time company came just one day after I finished my temporary admin job. It is a big-time company that is consistently voted as one of the Top 50 Best Employers of Canada. It has given me, not a big-time position, but big-time happiness.

The truth of the matter is, when you start seriously looking for a job, it would come. Minus the one year that I gallivanted, it took me only three months to get my first serious job. This was not without the support and encouragement of old and new friends, and a lot of wailing before the altar of the Lord.

Whatever your religious persuasion, the power of your prayers and your intercessors, both the living and the saints, will storm the mighty throne and open the windows of Heaven to grant you your heart's desire, in God's perfect time and perfect ways.

And only in continuing to believe that which you have not seen, and continuing to persevere, will you get to a desired destination in this your journey.

Just keep going. You will get there. That is as certain as the rainbow.

ATTRIBUTIONS AND SUGGESTED READINGS

Can You Start Monday? a 9-step job search, resume to interview
  by Cage, Cheryl A. c1998
Best Resumes for College Students and New Grads:
  jumpstart your career by Kursmark, Louise c2003
Getting the Job You Really Want: a step-by-step guide to finding
  a good job in less time by Farr, J. Michael c 2005
How to Find a Job after 50: from part-time to full-time, from
  career moves to new careers by Cummings, Betsy c 2005
How to Find a Job in Canada: common problems and effective
  solutions by Cheinis, Efim c2008
10 Insider's Secrets to a Winning Job Search: everything you need to
  get the job you want in 24 hours or less by Fujimoto, Sasushi c2005
The Procrastinator's Guide to the Job Hunt by Lanum, Lorelei c2004
What Color is Your Parachute? by Bolles, Richard Nelson

Resume Writing Workshop, Cornerstone Academy
   713-333 Terminal Ave. Vancouver BC V6A 2L7
Community Organizing and Leadership Training
   By Dr. Leonora C. Angeles, UBC Associate Professor
   Community and Regional Planning and Women's Studies

www.canadianimmigrant.ca
www.cfa.ca
www.fourinfo.com/volunteer
www.frannet.com
www.managementabout.com
www.mentoringprogram.com
www.quintcareers.com
www.statcan.gc.ca
www.wikipedia.org

And hundreds of other relevant internet websites and blogsites that make any modern-day author's search for information virtually easy and pretty straight-forward.